THE MAGIC OF
SPICE
BLENDS

THE MAGIC
— OF —
SPICE
BLENDS

A Guide to the Art,
Science, and Lore of
Combining Flavors

ALIZA GREEN

Quarto is the authority on a wide range of topics.

Quarto educates, entertains and enriches the lives of our readers—enthusiasts and lovers of hands-on living.

www.quartoknows.com

© 2016 by Quarto Publishing Group USA Inc.
Text © 2016 Aliza Green

First published in the United States of America in 2016 by
Quarry Books, an imprint of
Quarto Publishing Group USA Inc.
100 Cummings Center
Suite 406-L
Beverly, Massachusetts 01915-6101
Telephone: (978) 282-9590
Fax: (978) 283-2742
QuartoKnows.com
Visit our blogs at QuartoKnows.com.

10 9 8 7 6 5 4 3 2 1
ISBN: 978-1-63159-074-0

Digital edition published in 2016
eISBN: 978-1-62788-799-1

Library of Congress Cataloging-in-Publication Data available

Design: Samantha J. Bednarek
Photography: Steve Legato/stevelegato.com
Spezie Forti recipe, page 94, © 2014 Chef Cesare Casella

Printed in China

DEDICATION

THIS BOOK IS DEDICATED to my mother, Vivian Green, who introduced me to the magic of bustling markets, fresh ingredients, and bold spices. May she reach 100 years and more!

CONTENTS

◗ PREFACE

MAYBE IT WAS MY VISITS to spice markets in Mexico, Israel, Greece, and elsewhere—from childhood on—with their intoxicating smells and cone-shaped mounds of mysterious and colorful spices that first got me hooked on spices. Perhaps it's because of my inveterate curiosity about culinary ingredients. What is in this mysterious blend and what makes it smell so good? In my quest to learn more about spices, a trip to Greece led me to Elixir, a small shop in the wholesale market area of Athens with walls lined in antique wooden cabinets, each drawer filled with a different spice, dried bunches of potent Greek wild-harvested herbs hanging from the rafters, and mastica resin harvested only on the fragrant island known as Chios.

Getting to know the legendary Ann Wilder, founder of Baltimore's Vann's Spices, encouraged me to pursue my exploration of the world of spices and complex spice blends. On a trip to Napa Valley, California, I visited with spice maven, Shuli Madrone, who answered a slew of questions and introduced me to his select collection of spices. A few years later, I made a special trip to India to learn more about the world's biggest producer and consumer of spices and had the opportunity to spend an afternoon with a group of East Indian women who make their family heirloom–recipe, bottled masala, in giant batches once a year. My luggage was weighed down by bags (not nearly enough!) of their bottled masala and, best of all, a recipe to make it myself, which I have adapted for this book.

Several years ago, I had the pleasure of writing the small, compact *Field Guide to Herbs & Spices*, which whetted my appetite to learn more about spices: what happens when they are toasted, ground, and perfectly blended and how these blends provide the characteristic underlying flavor profile for world cuisine from Turkey to Morocco, Mexico to Thailand, Brazil to Sri Lanka. To test the recipes for this book and to hone my skills, I conducted a highly successful series of cooking classes focused on making spice blends and using them in recipes that I presented at the *Les Dames d'Escoffier* International annual conference, the Monell Chemical Senses Center, and at Baba Olga's Café in Philadelphia where I act as chef. Enthusiastic audience reaction further encouraged me to write this book.

Once I started working on it, everything just flowed and I got more and more immersed in the art of sourcing, roasting, and blending spices so that the finished mixture is so well-balanced that no one spice dominates, and the whole is far more than the sum of its individual parts.

Whether it's a blend of whole and crumbled spices for the highly adaptable Pickling Spice blend, a complex and intriguing mélange of Mediterranean, Indian, and East Asian spices for Moroccan Ras al Hanout; the Tunisian pantry staple, Harissa, which I learned to make from a Tunisian-Jewish restaurateur; or the Turkish basic blend, baharat, that my Turkish cooking friends rely on to season lamb kebobs and lahmajun, a spiced lamb flatbread, each of these blends brings a world of characteristic aromas into your kitchen for a quick and inexpensive mental get-away—that's the magic of spice blends!

So, until my next trip to Morocco or Turkey or Thailand or Mexico, I'll rely on my precious library of homemade spice blends to bring their characteristic flavors to my cooking. Once you've filled your home with the fragrance of toasting spices and start making your own blends, you'll be hooked, too.

AN INTRODUCTION TO
SPICES

There are various ways of categorizing spices, but five general categories are helpful: sweet, pungent, tart, hot, and savory. Many spices have elements of more than one category, so that habanero chiles are both hot (very hot!) and sweet and fruity, while coriander seeds are citrus-scented and the leaves, often known as cilantro, are highly pungent. Sweet spices include cinnamon, allspice, nutmeg, and vanilla. Pungent spices include star anise, licorice, cardamom, black cardamom, asafetida, mace, and clove, which may also have numbing qualities. Tart or tangy spices include sumac, ginger, tamarind, anardana and limu omani. Savory spices include many of the seeds and herbs such as coriander, fennel, parsley, oregano, rosemary, and mint.

In this chapter, we explore spices from several aspects: the various plant parts from which spices are derived and how they're produced; the terminology of grading and quality and how to make good choices; basic safety guidelines for handling and cooking with spices; and the essential techniques for working with them.

SPICES 101

PLANT PARTS AND BOTANICAL FAMILIES

Here I explain the various plant parts and families so that it's easy to understand why coriander, cumin, fennel, and anise work so well together—they are all part of the same Apiaceae family and share the same umbrella-shaped seedpod—and the relation between ginger, cardamom, galangal, and turmeric—they all derive from closely related rhizomes.

Spices are mostly derived from plant parts. A few come from animal-based sources, which appear at the end of the following list.

- **Bark:** true or Sri Lankan cinnamon, Chinese cassia, Indonesian cinnamon, Vietnamese cinnamon
- **Bulbs:** onion, garlic, shallot, chives
- **Flower buds and blossoms:** clove, caper, rose buds, nasturtium, orange blossom, hibiscus, kewra (screw pine blossom), lavender blossom, safflower (*Carthamus tinctorius*), saffron
- **Fruits:** anise, ajwain, black cumin (kala jeera), caraway, dill, coriander, cumin, fennel, celery, lovage (carom).

We call these members of the Apiaceae family "seeds," but they're actually tiny fruits.

- **Fruits (pods):** bell pepper, black cardamom, cardamom, hundreds of varieties of chile peppers, Sichuan pepper, Japanese sancho, star anise, tamarind, vanilla (fermented pods of the vanilla orchid)
- **Fruits (drupes and berries):** allspice (leaves also used), black peppercorns, Chinese wolfberry, cubeb pepper, Iranian barberry, bay laurel berries, lemon, lime, limu omani, kokam, long pepper, mango (unripe, dried, and powdered for amchur powder), orange, tangerine, pink peppercorn, sumac, juniper, wild lime fruit (also known as kaffir lime, a term now considered derogatory)
- **Leaf (only):** bay laurel, sassafras, curry leaf, Indian bay leaf, lemon myrtle, lemon verbena, Mexican pepperleaf, myrtle, screw pine leaf (pandanus), wild lime leaf (also known as kaffir lime)
- **Leaf and stems:** angelica leaves (golpar in Iran), basil, blue fenugreek, borage (blossoms are also eaten), celery, chervil, chives, cilantro, dill, epazote, fennel (another variety, Florence fennel, is cultivated for its enlarged bulbs), fenugreek leaves (methi in India), hyssop, lemon balm, lemongrass (stalks only), long coriander or culantro (Eryngium foetidum), lovage, Mexican tarragon (Tagetes lucida), marjoram, oregano, papalo (Mexico), parsley, spearmint, peppermint, perilla, rue, sorrel, sage, savory, tarragon, thyme, Vietnamese coriander, chepil (Mexico), and countless other herbs found in specific locales
- **Lichen:** stone flower (*Parmelia perlata*), also known as *kalpasi, kallupachi, chabila,* or *dagad phool* in Hindi
- **Pollen:** dill, wild fennel, cultivated fennel
- **Resin:** mastic, asafetida

- **Rhizomes:** galangal, ginger, turmeric, wasabi, zedoary (white turmeric)
- **Rind:** orange, lemon, lime, grapefruit, Omani lime, preserved lemon, preserved lime
- **Root:** angelica root (often candied for its decorative green color), celery root, coriander root, horseradish, licorice, parsley root
- **Seeds:** annatto, black and brown mustard, black sesame, blue poppy, cardamom, fenugreek, grains of paradise, mahlab cherry, white poppy, mace (outer covering of nutmeg seed), nigella, nutmeg, anardana (dried powdered pomegranate seeds or arils), white sesame, white or yellow mustard
- **Animal-derived seasonings:** blanchan or kapee (Southeast Asian and Indonesian fermented shrimp paste), fish sauce (Southeast Asian fermented anchovy liquid), colatura (Italian fermented anchovy sauce). Cantharidin (secreted by the emerald green beetle known as Spanish fly; now illegal in Morocco and elsewhere) sometimes added to ras al hanout for its supposed aphrodisiac qualities. The substance actually irritates the body's genitourinary tract, and can result in poisoning if ingested.

SPICE PRODUCTION

Most spices are grown in the tropical regions of the world, while many of the seeds used as spices come from temperate regions. The majority of spices are still harvested by hand, part of the reason for their high cost. The array of distinct and varied flavors in spices is contained in their volatile oils. Some of these flavors exist in spices in their fresh form, such as ginger, garlic, and chiles. These same spices taste different when dried, so that powdered ginger is hotter and less fruity than fresh ginger, and dried garlic is far more pungent than the fresh cloves.

They may be smoked for preservation, as in the case of black cardamom and many types of chiles, including Spanish pimentón and Mexican chipotles. Other spices must be dried and then fermented to bring out their flavor. These include vanilla, which is the tasteless green seedpod of the vanilla orchid until it has been fermented and turns black, and peppercorns, which turn black and pungent upon drying and fermenting.

▶ TOP TEN SPICE-PRODUCING COUNTRIES

India is by far the largest world spice producer, with 1,525,000 metric tons of spices produced in 2011, about 70 percent of world production. The next largest producer, Bangladesh, produced less than 10 percent of India's total. World spice production in 2011 was more than two million metric tons, which shows how important spices are to us.

According to the UN Food and Agriculture Organization, these are the top ten countries for world spice production in order from first to tenth:

1 India	5 Pakistan	8 Colombia
2 Bangladesh	6 Iran	9 Ethiopia
3 Turkey	7 Nepal	10 Sri Lanka
4 China		

GRADING AND QUALITY

When making your own spice blends, it's most important to start with high-quality, pure spices from a reputable supplier that preferably roasts and grinds their spices to order or in small batches. Because of their high value, spices have long been adulterated by various means. Valuable essential oils of a spice such as paprika or black pepper may have been removed and the remaining flavorless, spent spice used to extend the whole spice and save money.

Spices may be adulterated by having other, less valuable ingredients added for bulk, such as buckwheat or millet seeds added to ground black and white pepper, or coffee hulls added to ground cinnamon and nutmeg. Spices may be artificially colored by adding inexpensive turmeric to paprika, adding red food coloring to chili powder, adding tomato skins to paprika, or adding cistus leaves to oregano. These additions brighten and enhance color to appeal to consumers.

SPICES AND FOOD SAFETY

Many spices have antimicrobial properties, which helps explain why they are most commonly used in hot climates. Spices are often used to help preserve meat, fish, and poultry because these animal proteins are so susceptible to spoiling. Some of the earliest uses of spices and spice blends were to help preserve meats by making them into cured and dried sausages. Most herbs and spices are high in antioxidants, because of their flavonoids, which influence nutrition through many pathways, including affecting the absorption of other nutrients. Cumin, turmeric, and ginger are high in antioxidants, which also act as natural preservatives, preventing or slowing the rate of food spoilage.

Note that spices may be contaminated by salmonella bacteria, and this is the case for about 12 percent of the spices imported into the United States. To avoid possible illness, it's best to cook spices before using them by toasting in a dry skillet, frying in oil or other fat, or adding to simmering liquids such as soup. Cooking spices also enhances their flavor by freeing their essential oils. This is a common practice in countries with a large consumption of spices, such as Mexico and India, in moles and masalas.

Some spices, especially members of the chile family, may develop mold if they are exposed to high humidity. Others, especially those high in oils, such as sesame and poppy seeds, may develop insect damage, again if they are stored for long periods of time in a warm, humid place. Look for signs of insect eggs or clumping of dry spices and discard any spices that have been damaged. The oils in these seeds may also become rancid and should be discarded. Avoid these issues by storing spices in a cool, dark place in a tightly sealed container, or refrigerate or even freeze.

▶ BUYING SPICES AT INDIAN MARKETS

Indian markets are wonderful places to buy the most fragrant, pungent spices due to the far quicker turnover of product compared to jars and cans on supermarket shelves. Look for creamy white poppy; small, intense black cumin or kala jeera; deep yellow-orange Alleppey turmeric; and green, anise-like Lucknow fennel. This list of basic Indian spices with their Hindi names will help you negotiate the spice shelves at any Indian market.

SPICE	HINDI NAME
• Black Cumin	**Shahi Jeera**
• Black Peppercorns	**Kali Mirch**
• Cardamom	**Badi Or Kali Elaichi**
• Chickpea Flour	**Gram Flour**
• Cloves	**Lavang**
• Coriander Seeds	**Dhania**
• Cumin Seeds	**Jeera**
• Fennel Seeds	**Saunf**
• Fenugreek Seeds	**Methi**
• Indian Bay Leaves	**Tej Patta**
• Kashmiri Chiles	**Kashmiri Mirch**
• Mace	**Jaipatri**
• Mugwort	**Maipatri**
• Nutmeg	**Jaiphal**
• Poppy Seeds	**Post, Khus Khus**
• Sesame Seeds	**Gingelly**
• Star Anise	**Badian**
• Stone Flower Lichen, *Parmelia Perlata*	**Dagad Phool, Kalpasi, Kallupachi, Chab**
• True Cinnamon	**Darchini**
• Turmeric	**Haldi**
• Whole Wheat Flour	**Chapati Flour**
• Yellow Mustard Seeds	**Rai**

WORKING WITH SPICES AND HERBS

SOME SPICES ARE SOLD FRESH, especially near where they are grown, such as turmeric, ginger, galangal, mace, nutmeg, paprika, chiles, and even green peppercorns. But spices are most commonly sold in dried form, whole—best for long-keeping; crushed—best for mouth-pleasing texture and variety of color; or powdered—best for blending and even sprinkling, though this is their shortest-lived form. Because the volatile oils dissipate into the air, after a short time what is left of the original complex, multidimensional flavor are the harsher, longer-lasting elements. Compare the difference between store-bought ground black pepper and freshly ground black pepper or between store-bought ground nutmeg and freshly grated nutmeg.

The flavor of a spice derives partly from volatile oils that oxidize (react with oxygen) or evaporate when exposed to air. Grinding a spice greatly increases its surface area and so increases the rates of oxidation and evaporation. Some spices, like fenugreek, have fleeting aromas that quickly disappear after grinding. Whole dry spices will keep for two years or even longer without losing their volatile oils. Once ground, the spice will last up to six months, though spices such as paprika will lose their color and fade in flavor more quickly than that. It is best to store any spices away from the light. In fact, the old-fashioned tins used for some brands of spices, in which spices imported from India and Japan are often found, are the best way to store spices. The downside is that the spices can't be seen inside the tin.

The traditional way to grind whole spice is using a mortar and pestle. A microplane works well for grating nutmeg; a coffee grinder or special spice grinder is useful for amounts of less than 1 cup (225 g). We often use a heavy-duty blender with a strong motor to grind larger amounts of spice blends. Some spices may have their own dedicated mill, such as a pepper or salt mill, garlic press, or nutmeg grater.

The flavor elements in spices are soluble in oil, water, or alcohol (such as vanilla beans soaking in brandy or chile peppers soaking in sherry). Because the complex flavors of many spices take time to infuse into the food, most spices are added at the start of cooking. Some spices are so volatile that they are added at the end. Vanilla bean seeds and saffron, which is often soaked in a small amount of liquid to distribute its flavor and color better, are two examples.

▶ COOKING WITHOUT RECIPES

In addition to using spice blends in specific techniques and in recipes that reflect their regional origins there are many ways to use them in everyday ways, at a moment's notice.

- Use pizza or bread dough to make breadsticks. Brush or roll in olive oil, then roll in your choice of panch phoron, za'atar, vadouvan, berberé, or khmeli-suneli, and then bake.

- Brush flatbread with oil and sprinkle with the spice blends above, then bake until fragrant.

- Rub whole chicken with spice mix about an hour before roasting—use vadouvan, berberé, hawaij for soup, charmoula, Balti seasoning, chili powder, poultry seasoning, tabil or achiote paste.

- Add herb-based spice mixes such as khmeli-suneli, fines herbes, za'atar, nanami togarashi, or advieh to simple oil and vinegar or oil and lemon salad dressing.

- Add a pinch of sweet spice mix to dough for cookies such as oatmeal, blondies, shortbread cookies, and ground nut–based cookies such as Mexican or Greek wedding cookies. Use pumpkin pie spice, Chinese five spice, apple pie spice, or speculaas spice.

- Sprinkle steamed veggies with za'atar, khmeli-suneli, herbes de Provence, fines herbes, or tabil and serve with a wedge of lemon.

- Make a quick, healthy dip for veggies: combine plain Green yogurt with bottle masala, poudre de colombo, hawaij for soup, advieh, Balti seasoning, adobo, achiote paste, or Cajun seasoning. Allow the flavors to blend for about 30 minutes before serving.

- Rub steak, especially skirt, flank, tri-trip, or flat iron, with chili powder, berberé, Turkish baharat, or barbecue seasoning rub. Allow the steak to absorb the flavors at room temperature for 20 to 30 minutes, then broil, sear, or grill. Allow the steak to rest for 10 minutes, and then slice thinly against the grain.

- Love deviled eggs (and who doesn't)? Mix cooked yolks with a teaspoon or two of harissa, adobo, Brazilian tempero baiano, Yemenite hawaij or bottle masala, achiote paste, Cajun seasoning, or Old Bay and stuff into cooked whites. Sprinkle tops with a pinch of the spice. Do the same to perk up tuna salad or chicken salad.

DRYING FRESH HERBS

It's easy to dry herbs, especially when the humidity is low in winter. Home-dried herbs will be far more fragrant and appealing in color than the commercial type, which may have been sitting on the shelf for far too long. Rather than throwing out that spoiled bunch of fresh herbs, use half the bunch fresh and dry the remainder.

The best way to dry herbs, such as these spearmint leaves, is on the branch. Spread the stems out on a metal tray, preferably lined with parchment paper, and leave to dry at room temperature. Turn the stems after a few days so that they dry evenly. Or tie them into small bundles and hang to air-dry, which is best done indoors as bright sunlight will cause color fading and flavor loss. In humid climates, use an electric dehydrator, drying from 1 to 4 hours.

The herbs are fully dried when the leaves crumble easily and the small stems break when bent. Sturdy, resinous herbs such as sage, rosemary, oregano, thyme, and summer savory will dry most easily without a dehydrator.

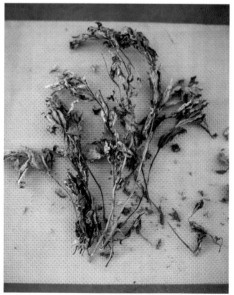

CREATING AN INDIAN-FLAVORED OIL

In this technique, which is known throughout the Indian Subcontinent as a *tarka* (see page 114), dry and fresh spices are fried in oil to release fragrant essential oils while enhancing flavor through browning. Another reason for frying the spices is to kill any salmonella bacteria by heating them. The spices, which are left whole, are added to the pan in order of cooking time, with dry spices first, followed by fresh, wet spices.

In addition to using a flavored oil as a topping for dal (see page 114) or other traditional Indian dishes, the mixture may also be used to flavor and enrich steamed vegetables, fish, cooked greens, potatoes, sweet potatoes, and grains such as wheat berries, buckwheat groats, barley, farro, quinoa, and corn.

1. Heat the oil (usually mustard, sesame, or coconut oil, or, as shown here, ghee or clarified butter) in a small, heavy skillet. Add the dry spices and fry briefly to brown lightly and release their aromas.

2. Add the wet spices (usually onion, garlic, ginger, and green chile) to the skillet. Fry briefly to release their aromas, then add the asafetida, which burns easily, and fry briefly.

3. Just before serving, season the dish as directed (dal, an Indian lentil dish, is shown here; see page 114), then spoon on the hot spiced oil mixture and garnish with chopped fresh herbs.

MAKING A SPICE-INFUSED PICKLING SYRUP

Pickling Spice adds its characteristic blend of herbal, aromatic, and savory flavors to pickled vegetables, mushrooms, meats such as corned beef, fish such as pickled herring and salmon, eggs, and fruit. Pickling Spices are kept whole so that the flavors penetrate the food. Ground spices would make the liquid cloudy and unappetizing. Because the spices are kept whole or in chunks, the flavors don't dissipate and the mixture will keep well up for to 8 months. Here we show how to make spiced sweet-and-sour syrup to pickle prune plums. (See page 90 for the complete recipe.) Pickling Spice is also used to make a marinade for the Beef Sauerbraten on page 91.

1. Have ready all the ingredients and combine as directed (see page 90). Use 1 to 2 tablespoons (7 to 14 g) pickling spice for each quart (L) of liquid. If desired, for easy removal, make a sachet by placing the pickling spices in cheesecloth and tying tightly with kitchen string, leaving a long "tail," which can be tied to the pot handle for easy removal.

2. Bring the water, sugars, vinegar, Pickling Spice, and other seasonings to a boil in a nonreactive (not aluminum) pot. Reduce the heat and simmer for 20 minutes to infuse the flavors.

3. If you are cooking fruit, prick each one in 2 or 3 places to keep them from bursting. Add to the liquid and cook for 3 minutes or until soft. Remove from the heat and cool to room temperature in the liquid. Transfer to storage containers, preferably glass, ceramic, or stainless steel, and refrigerate for 1 week to cure before serving.

SEASONING WITH A WET SPICE PASTE

Here we season a side of wild salmon with Vadouvan spice paste (see page 112 for the complete recipe). The mixture is spread in an even layer of the flesh side of the fish and roasted.

By adding salt and sugar, the Vadouvan spice paste can easily be made into a cure that penetrates the flesh of the fish and mixes with its natural juices to make brine. The liquid produced makes the fish firm and flavorful so that it may be sliced thinly like smoked salmon. To create a Vadouvan cure paste, combine the Vadouvan spice paste in the salmon recipe (page 112) with an additional 1 cup (134 g) kosher salt, and ¼ cup white (134 g) or brown (55 g) sugar. Spread the mixture evenly over the flesh side of the salmon and refrigerate for 4 to 6 hours.

OTHER SUGGESTED USES

Cube or slice veggies, toss with achiote paste, adobo, chermoula, berberé, poudre du colombo, or vadouvan, and then spread out in a single layer on a metal baking tray. Bake at 400°F (200°C, or gas mark 6) 20 to 30 minutes, until tender and browned on the edges.

ROASTING, GRINDING, AND STRAINING: CREATING SPICE BLENDS WITH CONSISTENT FLAVOR AND TEXTURE

This technique can be used to make Basic Curry Powder (see page 98), Ethiopian Berberé (page 36), Garam Masala (page 104), Hawaij (page 126), Jerk Seasoning (page 70), Khotachiwadi East Indian Bottle Masala (page 102), Poudre de Colombo (page 68), Ras el Hanout (page 26), and Sambar Podi (page 108). Shown here are the steps for making Balti Masala Spice Mix (see page 100).

1. Combine the hard spices (here, cassia, coriander, black cardamom, and cloves) in a large, heavy skillet. Toast over medium heat, while stirring with a wooden spoon. Remove spices from skillet and cool.

2. To the same skillet, add the smaller, softer seed spices (here, cumin, aniseed, black mustard, fenugreek, ajwain, and cardamom). Toast until the spices start to brown, keeping in mind that these spices can burn easily. Remove from the skillet and transfer the spices to a tray to cool.

3. Once the spices have cooled to room temperature, transfer to a large mortar and pestle (or use a heavy-duty blender or spice grinder). Crush the spices with the pestle by rubbing and mashing the spices against the sides and bottom of the mortar.

4. The finished spices should be in small, even chunks.

5. For even consistency, strain the spices through a wire sieve.

6. Combine with the remaining whole spices (here, nigella seeds).

SPICE AND HERB VOLUME TO METRIC WEIGHT CONVERSION CHART

While measuring spices by weight is certainly the most accurate way of measuring them, it's difficult to weigh small quantities unless you have a scientific gram scale. Use this chart to convert volume measurements (tablespoons) to grams (weight measurements) for accuracy when making larger amounts of spice blends.

1 TABLESPOON	GRAMS
• Dried Mint	4
• Dried Oregano	2
• Dried Rosemary	4
• Dried Tarragon	1
• Dried Thyme	6
• Garlic Powder	8
• Ground Aniseed	6
• Ground Bay Leaf	6
• Ground Caraway	6
• Ground Cardamom	6
• Ground Cayenne	8
• Ground Cinnamon (Cassia)	6
• Ground Cinnamon (True)	5
• Ground Clove	8
• Ground Coriander Seeds	6
• Ground Cumin Seeds	6
• Ground Fennel Seeds	6
• Ground Gingerroot	6
• Ground Mace	8
• Ground Nutmeg	8
• Ground Paprika	6
• Ground Star Anise	8
• Ground Turmeric	10
• Hot Red Pepper Flakes	12
• Rubbed Sage	4
• Table Salt	18
• Whole Black Peppercorns	8
• Whole White Peppercorns	10
• Whole Caraway Seeds	10
• Whole Cumin Seeds	10
• Whole Fennel Seeds	10

2

AFRICAN
BLENDS

In North Africa, the spice repertoire was influenced by the Moors, medieval Muslim inhabitants of the Maghreb (Morocco, Algeria, Tunisia, and Libya). Morocco's Ras el Hanout is based on warm seed spices such as cumin, fennel, caraway, and coriander and aromatic Asian spices such as ginger, cinnamon, cloves, and nutmeg. In southern Africa, the spice palate was influenced by European colonists and Indian and Malaysian immigrants. Arabic and Indian influences show up in Ethiopian Berberé. West African food is typically seasoned with fiery chiles such as lantern-shaped habaneros from the Caribbean, and tiny bird peppers, known as *piri piri* in Angola. Today, Nigeria is a major producer of ginger, while the islands off the coast of East Africa raise vanilla, allspice, and cloves for export. The most common African spices are cardamom, fresh and dried chiles, cilantro, cinnamon, cloves, cubeb pepper, long pepper, cumin, fenugreek, garlic, ginger, mint, nutmeg, sesame, and turmeric. Preserved lemons are a common seasoning in North Africa. Grains of paradise (related to ginger and turmeric) and tamarind are native to Africa and sesame may have originated there as well.

RAS EL HANOUT

Ras el Hanout, which means "head of the market" in Arabic, is a complex mélange of up to 100 spices that is basic to the cuisines of Morocco and other countries of the Maghreb (Morocco, Algeria, Tunisia, and Libya). This blend is full of subtle nuances from sweet spices such as cinnamon, cloves, and aniseed; hot spices such as black pepper and grains of paradise; and bitter spices such as turmeric and saffron, but no one spice dominates.

SPICEMASTER'S NOTE

In Morocco, ras el hanout seasons *mrouziya* (lamb stew with honey, raisins, and almonds) and *couscous t'faya* (chicken couscous with caramelized onions and raisins). It enhances lamb, meatballs, game birds (especially pigeon and guinea fowl), tagines, and couscous dishes, but isn't usually combined with fish, which would be overpowered by its flavor. It is essential to *b'stilla* (pigeon or chicken pie with almonds and cinnamon).

- ¼ cup (32 g) whole black peppercorns
- ¼ cup (40 g) whole white peppercorns
- ¼ cup (32 g) whole allspice berries
- ¼ cup (30 g) aniseed
- 2 large quills true cinnamon, lightly crushed
- 2 tablespoons (8 g) mace blades
- 2 tablespoons (20 g) decorticated cardamom
- 4 black (wild) cardamom pods, crushed (optional)
- 1 tablespoon (2 g) loosely packed saffron threads
- 2 whole nutmegs, grated
- ½ cup (48 g) ground ginger
- 6 tablespoons (60 g) turmeric
- ¼ cup (24 g) sweet paprika
- 2 teaspoons (6 g) ground cayenne pepper
- 2 tablespoons (8 g) dried edible rosebuds, petals removed and crushed (2 teaspoons [5 g] rosebud powder may be substituted)

1. Heat a dry skillet over medium heat. Add the black and white peppercorns, allspice, aniseed, cinnamon, mace, cardamom, and black cardamom. Toast, shaking often, until the spices are fragrant and lightly browned. Remove from the heat and immediately add the saffron to toast lightly.

2. Remove the spices from the skillet and cool to room temperature. Grind to a slightly coarse powder. Add the nutmeg, ginger, turmeric, paprika, cayenne, and crushed rosebud petals.

3. Transfer to a storage container and store, tightly covered, in a dark place for up to 6 months.

YIELD: About 3 cups (300 g)

CIGARI BOREKAS WITH SPICED LAMB FILLING

Borekas are small, easily portable filled pastries that came along with Turkey nomadic tribes in Central Asia when they moved westward from Anatolia. These pastries, found in many versions throughout the former Ottoman empire, may have sweet or savory fillings. Here we use Asian spring roll wrappers as a substitute for hard-to-find Moroccan *ouarka* or Tunisian *brik*; both thin-leaf pastry made by different methods. Turkish *yufka* dough is perfect, but the huge, folded rounds must be cut into 8-inch (20 cm) squares or 10-inch x 6-inch (25 x 15 cm) rectangles before filling. You may make the pastries and freeze and fry them directly from the freezer, allowing a little more cooking time.

FOR FILLING
- ¼ cup (60 ml) extra-virgin olive oil
- 2 medium onions, finely chopped
- 6 cloves garlic, finely chopped
- ¼ cup (25 g) Ras el Hanout
- 2 tablespoons (20 g) turmeric
- 2 pounds (908 g) ground lamb

- Salt and freshly ground black pepper, to taste
- 2 large eggs, lightly beaten
- ½ bunch Italian parsley, leaves and small stems chopped
- ½ bunch cilantro, leaves and small stems chopped

FOR ASSEMBLING

1 pound (454 g) square Asian
spring roll wrappers
(defrosted in the refrigerator if frozen)

1 large egg, lightly beaten with

1 tablespoon (15 ml) water,
for egg wash

3 cups (432 g) white sesame seeds

6 cups (1.4 L) olive oil or blended
vegetable and olive oil, for frying

TO MAKE THE FILLING:

1. In a large skillet, heat the olive oil.
Add the onion, garlic, Ras el Hanout, and
turmeric and cook until fragrant and the
onion is soft but not brown. Add the lamb,
salt, and pepper and cook, uncovered,
stirring occasionally, until the meat has
browned and the liquid in the pan has
evaporated, about 10 minutes.

2. Remove the pan from the heat and
drain off and discard any excess fat. Stir
in the eggs, cool to room temperature,
and then mix in the parsley and cilantro. To make the filling easier to work with, chill
until firm, about 30 minutes.

TO ASSEMBLE THE CIGARI:

1. Divide the filling into 24 equal portions. Line a baking sheet with parchment paper or
a silicone baking mat. Place 2 heaping tablespoons (30 g) of filling about 1 inch (2.5 cm)
above one end of a spring roll wrapper, spreading it out to make a cigar shape of filling,
with a 1-inch (2.5 cm) border on either end. Fold the bottom end over the filling, and then
lap the sides over it. Roll up tightly, making a tight cigar shape. Place the filled pastry seam-
side down on the baking sheet. Repeat until all the filling and wrappers have been used.

2. Have ready one bowl with the egg wash and a second bowl with the sesame seeds.
Dip the top of each pastry cigar into the egg wash, allowing the excess to drip off. Then,
dip the top of the pastry into the sesame seeds. Place the filled pastries, seam-side down,
back onto the baking sheet. The pastries may be frozen at this point.

3. Heat about half the oil in a large, heavy, cast-iron skillet or Dutch oven until
shimmering hot and the end of a wooden spoon dipped into the oil creates lively bubbles.
Note that the pan should be no more than one-third full of oil. Have ready a wire cooling
rack placed over a baking tray to catch the oil drips.

4. Carefully add about 6 cigari to the oil, one by one and sesame side down, so the pan is
full of pastries in a single layer. Fry until golden brown, 3 to 4 minutes, then carefully turn
using tongs and fry again until brown, 2 to 3 minutes. Remove the cigari using tongs or a
slotted spatula and transfer to the wire rack to drain. Repeat, adding more oil as needed,
until all the pastries have been fried.

5. Serve the cigari warm or at room temperature.

YIELD: 24 pastry cigars

OTHER SUGGESTED USES

Add to lamb stew, chicken stew, vegetable ragout, or lentil or chickpea soup.

Flavor sautéed mushrooms.

Rub lamb shoulder with Ras el Hanout, then slow-roast until fork-tender.

Marinate oily fish such as sardines, fresh tuna, salmon, and mahi-mahi in chermoula before grilling.

Spread the mixture all over and into slits cut into the skin of a whole fish such as branzino, red snapper, or black sea bass and then roast.

Roast cauliflower florets and drizzle with chermoula just before serving.

Dress steamed potatoes with chermoula for a Moroccan potato salad.

MOROCCO

CHERMOULA

Also found in Algeria and Tunisia, Chermoula is a tangy Moroccan seasoning paste that may be left chunky or blended until smooth. Tangy, bittersweet preserved lemon peel, acrid black nigella seeds, saffron, fresh cilantro, cumin, sweet aniseed, and rich, red paprika give the Chermoula its multifaceted, adaptable flavor. Chermoula pairs well with fish and seafood and enhances "meaty" vegetables such as okra, eggplant, mushrooms, cauliflower, and squash.

- 6 tablespoons (90 ml) extra-virgin olive oil, plus more for storing
- 2 lemons, juiced (about 6 tablespoons, or 90 ml)
- 1 small onion, finely diced
- ½ bunch cilantro, leaves and small stems chopped
- ½ bunch Italian parsley, leaves and small stems chopped
- 2 large cloves garlic, roughly chopped
- 1 preserved lemon, homemade or store-bought, yellow peel finely diced
- 3 tablespoons (21 g) sweet paprika
- 1 tablespoon (7 g) ground cumin
- 1 tablespoon (6 g) ground aniseed
- 2 teaspoons (6 g) nigella seeds
- 1 large pinch saffron threads
- 1 teaspoon hot red pepper flakes
- ½ teaspoon ground black pepper

Add all the ingredients to a medium bowl and whisk to combine. Transfer to a storage container and cover the chermoula with a thin layer of olive oil. Store refrigerated up to 3 weeks. Alternatively, combine all the ingredients except the nigella seeds in the jar of a blender and purée until smooth. Stir in the nigella and store.

YIELD: About 2 cups (400 g)

PRESERVED LEMONS

Preserved lemons are essential to North African cuisine, especially in tagines, where they combine well with green olives. Easy to make, the lemons are salted and cured in a process that takes about a month. The salty but tangy pulp can be used to season stews, mixed into sauces such as aioli or vinaigrette, or added to Bloody Mary mix.

- 12 large lemons, preferably organic
- 3 cups (864 g) kosher salt

1. Rinse the lemons in hot water. Quarter each from the top (nipple end) to within ½ inch (1.3 cm) of the bottom (stem end) and pull the quarters apart. Generously pack the exposed quarters with kosher salt, and then reshape the lemons. Place a layer of kosher salt on the bottom of a nonaluminum container. Add the lemons, pressing down to release their juices and to make room for more, adding more salt between the layers.

2. Cure at room temperature for 30 days, turning the container upside down occasionally to redistribute the salt and juices. As the lemons soften, syrupy juices will form; keep packing the lemons down and adding salt so that they are always covered with salt and/or juices. Store refrigerated after they have fully ripened.

3. To use, rinse the lemons as needed under cold water. Discard the salty inner pulp. Scrape off the inner white pith and discard. Slice, chop, or dice the rind to use in recipes.

YIELD: 12 preserved lemons

SPICY MOROCCAN STEAMED MUSSELS WITH CHERMOULA

The aromatic flavors of Morocco, with its coasts on both the Mediterranean and the Atlantic, accent the ocean essence of quick-cooking mussels in this meal in a pot enhanced by lemony Chermoula. Gold potatoes add appealing color and buttery richness. Serve with crusty bread to soak up the juices.

1   cup (200 g) Chermoula (page 28)
2   cups (500 g) chopped tomatoes, fresh or canned
1   teaspoon hot red pepper flakes (use more or less to taste)
2   cups (470 ml) water
1   pound (454 g) gold potatoes, cut into ½-inch (1.3 cm) cubes, peeled if desired

1   teaspoon sea salt
2   bags (4 pounds, or 1.8 kg) cultivated mussels
¼   cup chopped cilantro (4 g) or Italian parsley (15 g)

1. Heat the Chermoula in a large pot with a lid. Cook over medium heat while stirring until the spice mixture is sizzling and aromatic, about 1 minute. Add the chopped tomatoes, hot red pepper flakes, and water and bring to the boil. Add the potatoes and salt and bring back to a boil. Reduce heat and simmer until the potatoes are almost tender, about 10 minutes.

2. Meanwhile, place the mussels in a large bowl of cold water and swish around to rinse. Tap any mussels that have gaped open slightly. If they close, they're alive and safe to eat. Discard any that remain gaped open or that have broken shells. Add the mussels to the pot, cover, and steam open over high heat, about 5 minutes, shaking the pot several times. Discard any mussels that fail to open.

3. Add the cilantro and toss to combine, and then serve immediately, leaving behind the last cup (235 ml) or so of cooking liquid in case it contains any sand.

YIELD: 6 to 8 servings

TABIL

Tabil, pronounced "table," means "seasoning" in Tunisian Arabic and once referred simply to ground coriander, its main ingredient. Tabil is used together with Harissa Paste (page 32) to season meat and poultry stews, fish, preserved lamb, couscous with vegetables, and fried brik pastries. On its own it seasons the stuffing for vegetables and cooked vegetable salads. Some Tunisians prefer to use caraway seeds only without coriander. In Tunisia, the spices are pounded in a mortar and then dried in the sun. In humid climates, the spices are dried in a low oven.

SPICEMASTER'S NOTE

When working with fresh or dried hot chiles, it's a good idea to wear food gloves to keep your hands from absorbing the hot chile oil. Avoid breathing the fumes when chopping fresh hot chiles or wear a painter's mask. If you don't wear gloves, take extra care not to touch sensitive body parts with your hands.

6   whole dried chiles arbol or other similar dried hot red chiles
½   cup (40 g) coriander seeds
¼   cup (40 g) caraway seeds
1   head (about 14 cloves) garlic, peeled and minced
1   tablespoon (18 g) sea salt

1. Preheat the oven to the lowest temperature.
2. Remove the stems and seeds from the chiles, then crumble by hand (wearing food gloves) and reserve.
3. Combine the coriander and caraway seeds and grind to a slightly coarse powder in a spice grinder or blender. Mix together the spices, garlic, and salt and spread out in an even layer on a baking tray, then dry in the oven for 1 hour or until completely dry. Cool, combine with the crushed chile pepper, and then grind again to a slightly coarse powder.
4. Transfer to an airtight container and store in a cool, dark place for up to 4 months.

YIELD: About 2 cups (240 g)

TUNISIAN CARROT SALAD

Like many Tunisian salads, this one is based on a cooked vegetable, here carrots, mixed with aromatic seasonings and the fruity olive oil produced in Tunisia. In Tunisia, carrot salad such as this one (or a similar one made with zucchini) that has been mashed is used as a spread for casse-croûte sandwiches (page 33), making for a tasty alternative to high-fat mayonnaise. Because it is cooked, this salad will keep quite well for a week in the refrigerator, but allow it to come to room temperature before serving for best flavor.

2   pounds (908 g) carrots
3   cloves garlic, minced
6   tablespoons (90 ml) red wine vinegar
2   teaspoons (8 g) Harissa Paste (page 32)
2   tablespoons (15 g) Tabil
¼   bunch cilantro, leaves and small stems chopped
½   cup (120 ml) extra-virgin olive oil

1   Preserved Lemon (page 28), trimmed, white pith scraped off, and diced, for garnish
¼   cup (25 g) chopped oil-cured black olives
    Sea salt to taste
    Whole oil-cured black olives, for garnish
    Sprigs of cilantro, for garnish

Wash, peel, and dice the carrots. Boil in lightly salted water until tender, about 10 minutes. Drain and mix with the garlic, vinegar, harissa, Tabil, cilantro, oil, preserved lemon peel, chopped olives, and a little salt (the olives and preserved lemons are salty on their own). Garnish with whole olives and cilantro sprigs and serve.

YIELD: 6 to 8 servings

| **OTHER SUGGESTED USES** | Brush flatbread with olive oil, then sprinkle with Tabil and toast in the oven. | Sprinkle cubes of feta or other tangy white cheese with Tabil. | Drizzle sliced ripe tomatoes with extra-virgin olive oil, then sprinkle with Tabil. | Sprinkle quartered, hard-cooked eggs (leave them a little underdone) with sea salt and Tabil. |

HARISSA PASTE

Harissa, the basic hot and spicy seasoning paste of Tunisia, is served with kebabs and couscous in a small dish for diners to season as they wish. You can purchase premade harissa from Tunisia in tubes or cans, but the best is homemade without all the preservatives. In sun-soaked Tunisia, the red ripe peppers would be sun-dried.

- 3 pounds (1.4 kg) red bell peppers, roasted, peeled, and seeded
- 2 to 4 ounces (56 to 112 g) fresh hot red chiles, such as jalapeños or cherry peppers, seeded and trimmed
- 1 cup (96 g) pimentón (Spanish smoked paprika), dulce (sweet), or Spanish sweet paprika
- ½ cup (120 ml) extra-virgin olive oil, plus more for storing
- 8 cloves garlic, peeled
- ¼ cup (40 g) caraway seeds, ground in a spice grinder, or ¼ cup (40 g) ground caraway
- 2 tablespoons (36 g) fine sea salt

Combine all the ingredients in a food processor and process to a creamy, thick sauce. Transfer to a tightly sealed container, pour a layer of olive oil to cover the mixture to prevent mold from forming, and store in the refrigerator for up to 4 months.

YIELD: About 4 cups (800 g)

HARISSA SAUCE

Basic Harissa Paste is usually combined with other ingredients to make a thinner, pourable, and not quite as hot sauce to serve at the table. Instead of water, the liquid may be the cooking juices ladled from a tagine or stew.

- 2 tablespoons (30 g) Harissa Paste
- ¼ cup (60 ml) extra-virgin olive oil
- 1 tablespoon (4 g) chopped Italian parsley
- ½ cup (120 ml) cold water

Combine all the ingredients in a bowl and serve as a pourable sauce.

YIELD: About ¾ cup (150 g)

TUNISIAN CASSE-CROÛTE SANDWICH

Casse-croûte is a kind of hero sandwich filled with canned tuna, potatoes, tomatoes, egg, artichokes, and capers, served on a crusty French baguette and spiced with fiery harissa. Its name is adopted from the French who colonized Tunisia and means "break the crust." Feel free to spread the bread with mashed Tunisian Carrot Salad (page 30) for a milder, sweeter sandwich. This sandwich is best made with just-cooked potatoes that have not been refrigerated and rich olive oil–packed albacore or yellowfin tuna.

½ pound (227 g) Yukon gold potatoes, cut into ½-inch (1.3 cm) thick slices (peel if skin is thick)

1 crusty French baguette

¼ cup (60 ml) extra-virgin olive oil, divided

¼ cup (40 g) thinly sliced onion, preferably sweet onion

¼ cup (4 g) coarsely chopped cilantro

2 large ripe tomatoes, sliced

¾ cup (225 g) drained marinated artichokes, sliced if large

4 hard-cooked eggs, sliced (don't cook the eggs all the way through—they should be soft inside)

1 can (6 ounces, or 168 g) albacore or yellowfin tuna in olive oil, lightly drained and broken up

1 to 2 tablespoons (15 to 30 g) Harissa Paste (page 32)

4 tablespoons drained capers (34 g) and/or pitted and coarsely chopped cured black olives (25 g)

1 lemon, cut in half horizontally and seeds removed
Kosher salt and freshly ground black pepper to taste

1. Bring a small pot of salted water to a boil over high heat. Add the potatoes and cook until tender. Drain and allow the potatoes to cool but don't chill.

2. Slice the baguette horizontally to hinge without cutting all the way through. Pull out most of the soft bread from inside the top half of the baguette. Drizzle both sides with 2 tablespoons (30 ml) of the olive oil.

3. Sprinkle both sides of the bread with the sliced onion and cilantro. Shingle the tomato slices. Shingle the potatoes on the other side of the sandwich. Fill the center with the artichokes, sliced eggs, and tuna. Drizzle with the harissa.

4. Top with the capers and/or olives, and drizzle with the remaining 2 tablespoons (30 ml) olive oil. Squeeze the lemon over the top, then sprinkle the sandwich with salt and black pepper. Press the two sides of the sandwich together to compress, cut into 4 sections, and serve immediately or later the same day.

YIELD: 4 servings

OTHER SUGGESTED USES

Drizzle sliced avocado with lemon juice, olive oil, and Harissa Sauce.

Mix Harissa Sauce with the cooking juices from a chicken stew and pour back over the chicken before serving.

DUKKAH

Dukkah is an Egyptian blend of spices and roasted nuts that gets its name from a word meaning "to pound," as the ingredients are crushed together after being roasted to enhance their flavor. It is most commonly served with pita bread, which is dipped in fruity green olive oil and then in dukkah and eaten as a snack. Other ingredients that show up in dukkah (or dakka) are marjoram, mint, za'atar, chickpeas, cashews, and coconut. Dukkah also seasons lamb stew in Egypt and has become quite trendy in Australia because of immigrants from the Arabic world and a proliferation of television cooking shows.

1   cup (135 g) whole hazelnuts, skin on or off
1   cup (144 g) white sesame seeds
1   cup (145 g) pistachio meats
2   tablespoons (12 g) ground coriander
2   tablespoons (12 g) ground cumin
2   tablespoons (36 g) fine sea salt
2   teaspoons (4 g) ground black pepper

1. Preheat the oven to 325°F (170°C, or gas mark 3). Spread the hazelnuts on a baking pan and toast until light brown, about 12 minutes. If the hazelnuts have their skins on, cool them to room temperature and then remove the skins by placing the nuts in a clean towel, gathering the corners to make a kind of bag, and then rubbing off the flakes of skin. Pour off the nuts and discard the skins. (It's fine if a few pieces of skin remain.)

2. Separately, spread the sesame seeds on a baking pan and toast until light brown. Cool to room temperature. Chop the cooled hazelnuts and pistachios into small chunks by hand with a knife or in the food processor. Combine the nuts, sesame seeds, and spices.

3. Store the dukkah tightly covered, refrigerated or frozen, especially in hot weather, because the nuts can easily turn rancid.

YIELD: About 3½ cups (480 g)

PAN-FRIED HALLOUMI CHEESE WITH DUKKAH SPRINKLE

Halloumi, a specialty of Cyprus, is a brined cheese traditionally made from a mixture of goat and sheep's milk, though sometimes cow's milk is used in commercial versions. Because it is high in rennet, which coagulates cheese, and because the curd is cooked, this cheese doesn't melt when heated, so it is often fried or grilled. Like other Greek and Turkish cheeses, halloumi is stored in brine and also freezes well. It is often flavored with spearmint, which also acts as a preservative, very important in the days before refrigeration was common. When cooked, halloumi makes a squeaky sound as it is chewed. Here we pan-fry the cheese and top it with crunchy Dukkah for an easy mezze (Middle Eastern starter).

½ **pound (227 g) halloumi cheese, preferably goat and sheep's milk cheese**

2 **tablespoons (30 ml) extra-virgin olive oil**

½ **cup (70 g) Dukkah (page 34)**

1. Drain the halloumi and slice it into 4½-inch (11.4 cm) thick portions. Pat the cheese slabs dry with paper towels.

2. Heat the olive oil in a heavy skillet over medium heat. When it is just beginning to smoke, add the halloumi and cook for 2 minutes, or until well browned on the bottom. Turn the halloumi slabs over with a spatula, avoiding splashing the hot oil. Brown on the other side.

3. Transfer to serving plates. Sprinkle with the DDukkah and serve immediately.

YIELD: 4 servings

OTHER SUGGESTED USES

Use as a crunchy coating for chicken and fish fillets before roasting.

Sprinkle over green salad, hummus, or baba ghanoush just before serving.

Sprinkle on Greek yogurt, drizzled first with extra-virgin olive oil, for a savory snack.

ETHIOPIA

BERBERÉ

Berberé is the Amharic name for a spice mixture that is a basic flavoring in Ethiopia and nearby Eritrea. This highly aromatic and extremely hot spice mixture is a blend of Arabic and Indian flavors and has a coarse, earthy texture. Berberé is essential to the family of Ethiopian stews called *wats*, made with meats, fish, chicken, legumes, and vegetables. It may include plants that grow wild in Ethiopia such as korarima (a cousin to cardamom and ginger) and long pepper (a cousin to black pepper) as well as aromatic fenugreek, a type of legume, and ajwain (or carom seeds), which resembles small caraway seeds and has a flavor like concentrated thyme. Long pepper and chiles add pungency, and cassia, cardamom, and allspice add sweet aroma. Note that decorticated cardamom is the inner cardamom seeds with the outer pod shell, usually white or green, removed. This recipe is rounded and warm in flavor with medium heat so that it blends well in many recipes.

2 tablespoons (12 g) fenugreek seeds
¼ cup (24 g) coriander seeds
2 tablespoons (12 g) cumin seeds
4 teaspoons (8 g) ajwain (carom seeds)
1 piece (2-inches, or 5 cm) cassia cinnamon quill
6 long pepper pods or 2 tablespoons (16 g) black peppercorns
2 teaspoons (6 g) whole allspice berries
1 tablespoon (10 g) decorticated cardamom
2 tablespoons (20 g) ground turmeric
2 tablespoons (12 g) ground ginger
2 teaspoons (6 g) ground or freshly grated nutmeg
2 tablespoons (12 g) paprika
8 crushed bird's eye chiles or 1 tablespoon (8 g) ground cayenne or other powdered hot chile
1 teaspoon ground cloves
¼ cup (72 g) kosher salt

1. In a dry skillet over medium heat, toast the fenugreek, coriander, cumin, and ajwain until fragrant and lightly browned, shaking the pan so spices toast evenly. Remove from the skillet, cool to room temperature, and reserve.

2. Crush the cinnamon into small pieces with a meat mallet or a hammer. Heat a dry skillet over medium heat. Add the long pepper, allspice berries, crushed cinnamon, and cardamom seeds and toast until fragrant and lightly browned, shaking frequently so the spices toast evenly. Remove from the skillet, cool to room temperature, and reserve.

3. Combine the toasted spices and grind or crush to a slightly coarse powder. Mix the ground toasted spices with the turmeric, ginger, nutmeg, paprika, chiles, cloves, and salt.

4. Store the berberé in a tightly sealed container in a dark place for up to 4 months.

YIELD: About 1½ cups (135 g)

How to tell if you have true cinnamon: It's rolled up like a rug and is friable and pale pinkish beige. Its cousin, the coarser, more peppery cassia, is rolled from both sides like a Torah scroll is woody and deep reddish brown and very hard.

ETHIOPIAN LENTIL STEW WITH BERBERÉ

The mellow flavors of berberé blend exceptionally well with legumes such as chickpeas, lentils, and common beans. The kick of the aftertaste brings these sometimes stodgy legumes to life. Here we use French green lentils because of their firm texture and nutty flavor. These lentils will hold their shape when cooked and don't turn mushy or mealy like common brown or green lentils, which are better for soup.

1	pound (454 g) French green lentils	2	tablespoons (16 g) grated fresh gingerroot
6	cups (1.4 L) water		
	Salt to taste	4	cloves garlic, minced
1	large yellow onion, finely diced	2	tablespoons (16 g) Berberé (page 36)
2	carrots, finely diced	2	cups (360 g) chopped plum tomatoes
¼	cup (60 ml) vegetable oil	½	cup (30 g) chopped flat-leaf parsley

1. Place the lentils and water in a medium pot and bring to a boil over high heat. Reduce the heat to low and simmer for 20 minutes, then add the salt and continue cooking for 20 to 25 minutes, or until the lentils are tender but not mushy, skimming off white foam as necessary.

2. Meanwhile, in a large Dutch oven, sauté the onion and carrot in the oil until softened, about 5 minutes. Add the ginger, garlic, and berberé spice and sauté several minutes longer, or until fragrant. Add the tomatoes, bring to a boil, and simmer for 10 minutes. Drain the lentils and add to the pot. Simmer for 10 minutes to combine flavors, season with more salt, parsley, and serve.

YIELD: 8 servings

ASIAN
BLENDS

The immense and diverse region of East Asia is dominated by Chinese culture. Its main typical spice blend is five-spice powder. Chinese cinnamon (cassia), ginger, lesser galangal, perilla, Sichuan pepper, star anise, wasabi, and water pepper are all native to this region. In Japan, two related spice blends, Shichimi Togarashi and nanami togarashi, are found. Shichimi Togarashi, or seven spice *shichi* ("seven" in Japanese), contains ground red chile, Japanese sancho, tangerine peel, nori (dried seaweed), white poppy, black hemp or black sesame, and garlic. Nanami togarashi is similar but emphasizes citrus zest.

Many of the world's most prized spices are indigenous to tropical Southeast Asia, including cloves, cubeb pepper, galangal, Indonesian cinnamon, wild lime, lemongrass, long pepper, mace, nutmeg, and Vietnamese coriander. The sweet spices such as cinnamon, cloves, nutmeg, and mace are mostly exported, while the others are essential to the region's numerous fresh curry pastes.

SHICHIMI TOGARASHI

Togarashi, the Japanese word for "chiles," is a group of chile condiments that bring out the clean, simple flavors of Japanese food. Shichimi Togarashi is also called Japanese seven spice because seven ingredients are generally used. It works well with fatty foods such as unagi (broiled eel), tempura-fried foods, shabu shabu (small bits of food cooked in rich broth), noodle dishes, and yakitori (grilled dishes). Nanami togarashi is a close cousin. Nori is sheets of dried seaweed, made by a process that resembles papermaking and is available in Asian markets.

<table>
<tr><td>¼</td><td>cup Japanese sancho (20 g) or Sichuan peppercorns (36 g)</td><td>4</td><td>teaspoons (10 g) white poppy seeds (substitute black hemp seeds, if available, or white sesame seeds)</td></tr>
<tr><td>2</td><td>tablespoons (12 g) dried tangerine (or orange) peel</td><td></td><td></td></tr>
<tr><td>4</td><td>teaspoons (2 g) crushed, flaked nori</td><td>2</td><td>tablespoons (16 g) ground dried red chile powder, such as cayenne</td></tr>
<tr><td>4</td><td>teaspoons (11 g) black sesame seeds</td><td>4</td><td>teaspoons (12 g) granulated garlic</td></tr>
</table>

1. Heat a dry skillet over medium heat. Add the sancho or Sichuan peppercorns and toast until fragrant, about 1 minute. Remove from the pan and reserve.

2. Using the same skillet, toast the tangerine peel, nori, sesame seeds, and poppy seeds for about 1 minute, or until fragrant. Remove from the pan and reserve.

3. Using the same skillet, toast the chile powder over medium heat for 30 seconds. Cool and then combine with the toasted spices and the garlic.

4. Grind all together to a chunky consistency. Store in an airtight container, refrigerated, for up to 1 month.

YIELD: About 1 cup (100 g)

JAPANESE UDON NOODLES WITH SHICHIMI TOGARASHI

Udon noodles are thick, smooth, chewy wheat flour noodles usually served in soup. Here we combine the noodles with smoky shiitake mushrooms and juicy bok choy. A last-minute sprinkling of shichimi togarashi, roasted peanuts, and scallions adds a burst of flavor and welcome crunchy texture. Serve the noodles in large Asian-style soup bowls for a one-dish, vegan-friendly meal.

<table>
<tr><td>½</td><td>pound (227 g) fresh shiitake mushrooms</td><td>1</td><td>tablespoon (15 ml) rice vinegar</td></tr>
<tr><td>1</td><td>small head baby bok choy</td><td>1</td><td>tablespoon (15 ml) Japanese toasted sesame oil</td></tr>
<tr><td>1</td><td>cup (75 g) snow peas</td><td></td><td></td></tr>
<tr><td>1</td><td>package (1 pound, or 454 g) fresh or precooked udon noodles</td><td>1</td><td>teaspoon Shichimi Togarashi</td></tr>
<tr><td>2</td><td>tablespoons (30 ml) vegetable oil, divided</td><td>3</td><td>tablespoons (27 g) chopped roasted salted peanuts</td></tr>
<tr><td>¼</td><td>cup (60 ml) soy sauce</td><td colspan="2">3 or 4 scallions, thinly sliced</td></tr>
</table>

1. Remove the stems from the shiitakes and reserve, if desired, for another use, such as mushroom stock. Slice the caps thinly and reserve. Trim the bok choy, slice thinly, and reserve. Cut the snow peas into thin julienne strips and reserve.

2. When ready to finish the dish, bring a medium pot of salted water to a boil. Cook the fresh udon noodles for about 2 minutes, or until just tender, then drain and reserve. If using precooked noodles, dip the udon into the boiling water for 30 seconds to soften and then drain.

3. Meanwhile, heat 1 tablespoon (15 ml) of the oil over high heat in a wok or large skillet. Add the shiitakes and sauté until crisp-tender, shaking the pan frequently. Remove from the pan, add the snow peas, stir to wilt lightly, and reserve. Repeat with the remaining 1 tablespoon (15 ml) oil and the bok choy and remove from the skillet. Add the noodles, soy sauce, vinegar, and sesame oil to the pan and heat to boiling, shaking to combine. At the last minute, toss with the shiitakes, bok choy, and snow peas.

4. Transfer the noodles mixture to individual serving bowls. Sprinkle with the Shichimi Togarashi, peanuts, and scallions and serve piping hot.

YIELD: 4 to 6 servings

GOMASIO

Gomasio is a simple Japanese sesame and sea salt mix also found in Korea. Classically, it is made using a special Japanese grooved ceramic mortar with a wooden pestle called a *suribachi*. It is an essential seasoning in the Japanese-based macrobiotic cooking. In Japan, *gomasio* is an idiomatic term for someone with mixed white and black hair, similar to the English "salt and pepper" hair. It always accompanies osekihan, Japanese adzuki beans and rice.

¼ cup (72 g) fine sea salt

3 cups (432 g) sesame seeds, either white (hulled) or natural brown

1. Heat a dry skillet over medium heat until almost smoking. Add the salt and roast until the salt turns gray in color. Remove from the pan and reserve. Add the sesame seeds to the same pan and toast over low heat until the seeds are fragrant, evenly browned, and start to pop, shaking the pan often. Remove from the pan and keep stirring until the popping stops. Cool to room temperature.

2. Combine the roasted salt and sesame seeds and either process in a spice grinder to a slightly chunky consistency or crush in a mortar and pestle. The gomasio should be light and sandy, not oily or pasty.

3. Store in a tightly closed container, preferably glass or tin, and keep in a cool, dry place for up to 1 month.

YIELD: About 3 cups (528 g)

OTHER SUGGESTED USES

Sprinkle on steamed fish, steamed vegetables, or rice.

Use to season green and vegetable salads.

JAPANESE CHICKEN MEATBALL SKEWERS WITH GOMASIO SPRINKLE

These tender meatballs with their savory-sweet glaze work well as a party appetizer or served over steamed rice for a main dish. Prepare the meatballs and skewers up to two days before grilling, keeping them covered and refrigerated until ready to cook. Dark meat chicken will have the best flavor and enough fat to keep the meatballs moist, but it's important to choose top-quality chicken, preferably grain-fed, for its milder, nutty flavor. A final sprinkle of Gomasio and sliced scallions lends nutty flavor and contrasting texture.

FOR GLAZE

¼ cup (60 ml) cup soy sauce
¼ cup (60 ml) mirin
2 tablespoons (30 ml) rice vinegar
2 tablespoons (12 g) chopped fresh gingerroot
1 large clove garlic, chopped
2 teaspoons (6 g) whole white peppercorns
¼ teaspoon chile oil or ground cayenne

FOR MEATBALLS

2 pounds (908 g) ground chicken, preferably dark meat
1 egg white
¾ cup (83 g) Japanese panko breadcrumbs
1 large shallot, minced
2 tablespoons (12 g) chopped fresh gingerroot
1 large clove garlic, minced
1 teaspoon sea salt
½ teaspoon ground white pepper
1 tablespoon (15 ml) Japanese roasted sesame oil
  Oil, for the grill

¼ cup (44 g) Gomasio
½ bunch scallions, thinly sliced

TO MAKE THE GLAZE:

1. In a small saucepan, combine the soy sauce, mirin, vinegar, ginger, garlic, and peppercorns and bring to a boil. Cook over medium heat until the sauce has thickened, 5 to 10 minutes. Remove from the heat, strain through a wire sieve, add the chile oil, and reserve.

TO MAKE THE MEATBALLS:

1. Soak sixteen 8-inch (20 cm) bamboo skewers in water to cover for at least 30 minutes.
2. Combine the meatball ingredients (through the sesame oil) in a large bowl and mix well by hand. Form the mixture into 32 meatballs. Thread the meatballs onto the skewers, without crowding. Flatten each meatball to make a puck shape. Arrange the skewers on a parchment- or wax paper–lined tray. Reserve, refrigerated, until ready to grill.
3. Preheat a grill with a cover until no fire remains, just white coals. Prepare the grate by wiping with a paper towel soaked in a little vegetable oil. Grill the skewers indirectly until grill marks form, then turn over and grill until the meatballs are cooked through but still juicy. Brush with the glaze while grilling, then turn over and repeat, grilling for about 4 minutes on each side.
4. Alternatively, preheat the oven to 350°F (180°C, or gas mark 4) and preheat a large cast-iron skillet or grill pan. Sear the skewers on the stove top, brush all sides with glaze, then finish in the oven until cooked through.
5. Transfer the skewers to a platter, sprinkle with the Gomasio and sliced scallions, and serve immediately.

YIELD: 8 servings

FIVE-SPICE POWDER

This highly aromatic sweet-spicy mixture enhances beef, chicken, noodle dishes, and especially fatty meats such as pork and duck. Five-spice powder is quite potent, so be judicious. The blend is a culinary cousin to French Quatre Épices (page 80), though the two developed independently. Some versions include ground licorice root and ginger.

½ **cup (30 g) whole star anise pods**
½ **cup (80 g) fennel seeds**
3 **tablespoons (24 g) Sichuan peppercorns**

2 **tablespoons (12 g) crushed cassia cinnamon quills**
2 **teaspoons (3 g) whole cloves**

Combine all the spices and grind or crush to a fine powder in a spice grinder or mortar and pestle.

YIELD: About 1¼ cups (144 g)

SPICEMASTER'S NOTE

Use a hammer or mallet to crush whole cassia cinnamon quills into smaller pieces. One 3-inch (7.5 cm) quill will yield about 2 tablespoons (12 g).

VIETNAMESE CHICKEN BAHN-MI SANDWICH WITH CHINESE FIVE SPICE

This classic Vietnamese sandwich is a legacy of the years of French colonialism in Indochina and combines French ingredients such as baguette bread, butter lettuce, and mayonnaise with Vietnamese ingredients such as fish sauce, Vietnamese basil, pickled daikon, and Chinese Five-Spice Powder to season the chicken. In Vietnam, the sandwich is usually served on a single-serving soft baguette with pointed ends and thinner crust than French-style baguettes. A hero, submarine, or hoagie roll makes a good substitute.

½	cup (120 g) mayonnaise, homemade or store-bought	1	recipe Spiced Chicken for Banh Mi, sliced
2	French baguettes, split open horizontally	1	recipe Marinated Daikon and Carrots
		1	large handful fresh cilantro leaves
3	jalapeño chiles, sliced lengthwise paper thin, seeds removed	1	large handful Vietnamese or Thai basil, or mint leaves
½	sweet onion, sliced paper thin	1	head butter lettuce, leaves picked
1	cucumber, preferably seedless, cut into long spears		

1. Spread a thin layer of mayonnaise on the bottom layer of bread and top with the chiles, onion, and cucumber.

2. Arrange the sliced chicken on top. Top with the marinated daikon and carrots, cilantro, basil, and lettuce. Spread the top layer of bread with a thin layer of mayonnaise.

3. Close the sandwich, press together to compress, and cut into 4 sections for each loaf. Secure with toothpicks and serve.

YIELD: 6 to 8 servings

SPICED CHICKEN FOR BANH MI

2	pounds (908 g) boneless, skinless chicken thighs, trimmed of excess fat	2	cloves garlic, minced
		2	tablespoons (25 g) sugar
¼	cup (60 ml) vegetable oil	1	tablespoon (7 g) Five-Spice Powder (page 44)
¼	cup (60 ml) soy sauce		

In a bowl, combine the chicken with the remaining ingredients and marinate for at least 2 hours. Drain, discarding the marinade. Heat a large, heavy-bottomed skillet, such as cast iron, then pan-sear the chicken on both sides until thoroughly cooked. Cool and slice thinly against the grain.

YIELD: 2 pounds (908 g), enough for 8 sandwiches

MARINATED DAIKON AND CARROTS

1	large daikon root, peeled	2	tablespoons (25 g) sugar
½	pound (227 g) carrots, peeled	2	teaspoons (12 g) kosher salt
¾	cup (180 ml) rice vinegar		

Julienne-cut the daikon and carrot into matchsticks using a French or Japanese mandoline. Add to a bowl. Whisk together the vinegar, sugar, and salt. Toss half the marinade with the vegetables, reserving the remainder. Allow the vegetables to marinate, stirring occasionally, for 30 minutes. Drain in a colander and combine with the remaining half of the marinade. Reserve.

YIELD: 1 pound (454 g), enough for 8 sandwiches

OTHER SUGGESTED USES

Add to braised beef short ribs with tomato and soy.

Add to stir-fry sauces.

Rub pork tenderloin with oil, salt, and Five-Spice Powder before roasting.

Add to dumpling filling, especially beef, pork, cabbage, or mushrooms.

THAI CURRY PASTES

Thai curry pastes are a highly fragrant mélange of pungent dried fish or fish sauce (fermented anchovy liquid) and fermented shrimp paste ground with fresh green chiles, fragrant leaves and zests (lemongrass, coriander, Thai basil, wild lime leaf, and the grated zest of the bumpy wild lime fruit), rhizomes (galangal, turmeric, and fingerroot—a somewhat medicinal tasting finger-shaped rhizome, which is widely used in the Javanese cuisine of Indonesia), and members of the allium family (especially pink shallots and garlic). Yellow or Massaman curry paste comes from the south of Thailand near Malaysia. It has a strong Indian influence in the use of spices such as cardamom and cloves. It usually contains coconut, roasted peanuts or cashews, cardamom pods, star anise, palm sugar, fish sauce, chiles, and tamarind. Green curry paste is usually the hottest because of all the fresh green chiles it contains. Red curry paste is full-bodied, fragrant, and milder.

THAI RED CURRY PASTE

The galangal (or galingale) called for here is a first cousin to ginger and an important seasoning in Southeast Asian cooking, used to flavor curries, soups, and stews. It is more pungent than ginger, with a sharper bite and a tangy flavor reminiscent of hot mustard. Fresh galangal is occasionally found in natural foods and Asian markets, and may also be called *laos* (its Indonesian name). Substitute fresh gingerroot if galangal is not available.

4 dried New Mexico chiles (substitute dried mild red chiles such as ancho or California)
6 dried whole small hot red chiles (such as arbol or bird's eye)
2 tablespoons (10 g) coriander seeds
2 tablespoons (30 ml) vegetable oil
½ cup (80 g) chopped shallots
¼ cup (40 g) sliced garlic
4 to 6 wild lime leaves, or the zest of wild lime fruit or lime
1 large stalk lemongrass, tough outer layers discarded, thinly sliced

1 section (2 inches, or 5 cm) fresh galangal or gingerroot, peeled and chopped
1 small handful cilantro root (optional but very good; look for this in Asian markets)
1 piece (1 inch, or 2.5 cm) fresh turmeric root (sold in season in Asian markets) or 1 tablespoon (10 g) ground turmeric
2 tablespoons (30 g) Thai shrimp paste
1 lime or wild lime, juiced
1 tablespoon (12 g) sugar
2 teaspoons (12 g) fine sea salt

1. Trim both kinds of chiles and discard the stems and seeds. Soak the chiles in warm water to cover until soft and pliable, about 30 minutes.

2. Heat a skillet over medium heat without any oil. Add the coriander seeds and toast until lightly browned and fragrant. Remove from the skillet, cool to room temperature, and grind to a slightly chunky powder. In the same skillet, heat the oil and cook the shallots and sliced garlic over moderate heat until lightly browned, about 8 minutes, stirring often.

3. Combine the wild lime leaves, lemongrass, galangal, cilantro root, and turmeric root and finely mince together.

4. Drain the chiles, reserving the liquid. Using a food processor, purée the chiles to a chunky paste, and then add the ground coriander, shrimp paste, roasted shallots and garlic, and the wild lime mixture, adding about 1 cup (235 ml) of the reserved chile soaking liquid as needed to process.

5. Remove the mixture from the processor and add the lime juice, sugar, and sea salt. Transfer to a tightly sealed container and store, refrigerated, for up to 1 month.

YIELD: About 3 cups (750 g)

SPICEMASTER'S NOTE

If desired, freeze the curry paste in ice cube trays. Once frozen, transfer the frozen curry paste cubes to a tightly sealed container and store frozen for up to 4 months. This is an easy way to use just as much curry paste as needed.

OTHER SUGGESTED USES

Use to season fish, shellfish, chicken, and vegetable curries.

Finish with rich unsweetened coconut milk for a creamy, nondairy sauce.

Add a tablespoon or two (15 to 30 g) to mayonnaise and use as a dip for vegetable crudités or crunchy fried-shrimp crackers.

THAI SCALLOPS IN COCONUT-RED CURRY SAUCE

This impressive, quickly prepared meal accents dense, sweet sea scallops with warm, spicy red curry paste scented with orange zest. Chicken breast cubes, shrimp, or firm fish, such as albacore tuna or swordfish, make good substitutes. The potent flavor of the red curry paste is tempered with coconut cream to produce a rosy-pink sauce that's aromatic and spicy but not too fiery.

3   shallots, finely chopped

1   section (2 inches, or 5 cm) fresh galangal (substitute ginger), peeled and grated

4   tablespoons (60 ml) vegetable oil, divided

¼   cup (62 g) Thai Red Curry Paste (page 47)

1   orange or tangerine, zested and juiced

1   cup (235 ml) rich unsweetened coconut cream
Sea salt and ground white pepper

2   pounds (908 g) large sea scallops, trimmed of hard side muscle

1   handful Thai basil, leaves shredded (or substitute basil mixed with mint)

1   bunch scallions, sliced on the diagonal
Jasmine rice, for serving

1. In a medium skillet over low heat, cook the shallots and galangal in 2 tablespoons (30 ml) of the oil until softened, about 10 minutes. Stir in the Thai Red Curry Paste and cook until fragrant, about 2 minutes, stirring constantly. Add the orange zest and juice, coconut cream, and salt to taste. Bring to a boil, reduce the heat, and simmer until the liquid is slightly reduced and thickened. Reserve.

2. Heat the remaining 2 tablespoons (30 ml) oil in a wok or large skillet over high heat until it shimmers. Season the scallops with ½ teaspoon salt and a large pinch of pepper. Add the scallops to the pan and sear on one side until browned, then turn over and sear again until barely opaque, about 3 minutes total.

3. Stir the Thai basil into the curry sauce and spoon onto serving plates. Arrange the scallops on top, sprinkle with the scallions, and serve immediately accompanied by cooked jasmine rice.

YIELD: 4 servings

THAI GREEN CURRY PASTE

This fresh-tasting curry paste gets its heat from lots of small hot green chiles; its fragrance from lemongrass and lots of fresh green herbs such as cilantro, mint, and Thai basil; its earthiness from shallots and garlic; its pungency from fish sauce and shrimp paste; and its slightly medicinal pungency from galangal root. Though unrelated, its green heat is reminiscent of spicy green Yemenite Zhoug (page 128).

3 stalks lemongrass, inner layers minced (see "How to Prepare Lemongrass," below)
6 Thai green chiles, seeded and thinly sliced
4 serrano or 2 jalapeño chiles, seeded and thinly sliced
4 large shallots, sliced
6 large cloves garlic, sliced
2-inch (5 cm) section fresh galangal or gingerroot, grated (about 2 ounces, or 56 g)
¼ cup (30 g) chopped cilantro roots (optional, available in Asian markets)

1 bunch cilantro, leaves plus small stems, chopped
1 bunch Thai basil, leaves plus small stems, chopped
1 bunch spearmint leaves, chopped
1 tablespoon (6 g) ground cumin
1 tablespoon (6 g) ground coriander
6 tablespoons (90 ml) Asian fish sauce
1 tablespoon (15 g) Asian shrimp paste
2 teaspoons (4 g) ground white pepper
2 wild limes, zested and juiced (available in Thai markets) or juice and grated zest of 1 lime

Place all the ingredients in a food processor, chopper, or blender and process to form a thick, chunky paste. Store in a tightly sealed container, refrigerated, for up to 2 weeks, or freeze for up to 3 months.

YIELD: About 2 cups (500 g)

▶ HOW TO PREPARE LEMONGRASS

Choose moist, fragrant lemongrass stalks that are firm, full, and pale green in color—an indication of freshness. To prepare lemongrass, wash and then trim off the root ends with a sharp knife. Peel off and discard two or three woody outer layers or add to soup stock. Use only the relatively tender heart of the stalk—4 to 6 inches (10 to 15 cm) from the bottom up to the point where the leaves start to branch out. (If the lemongrass is very dry, soak in warm water.)

Smash the trimmed lemongrass stalks with a mallet or the side of a heavy knife to release the essential oils. Add to soup broths and other liquids to infuse, and remove before serving. Thinly slice tender inner hearts and then chop finely by hand or in the food processor. (You must slice the lemongrass before processing to cut the fibers.) Wrap whole or trimmed lemongrass tightly with foil or plastic wrap and store for up to 2 weeks in the refrigerator, or freeze chopped lemongrass in a tightly sealed container for up to 3 months.

OTHER SUGGESTED USES

Add to a curry sauce with chicken, pork, beef, tofu, mushrooms, potatoes, or vegetables cooked in a little oil. Add liquid (water or stock) and simmer together until fully cooked. Just before serving, swirl in rich unsweetened coconut milk.

Add a tablespoon or two (15 to 30 g) to mayonnaise and use to dip vegetable crudités.

Add a spoonful to chicken, tuna, or roasted eggplant salad.

THAI LEMONGRASS SHRIMP

This quick-cooking dish is infused with Thai flavors of lemongrass, ginger, and hot, herbal green curry paste. Now that Asian ingredients such as fresh lemongrass, coconut cream, and gingerroot are easily found even at the supermarket, this fragrant sauté is easy to make. Choose wild American white or pink shrimp or Mexican white shrimp for firm texture and sweet flavor. Avoid stronger and mushier black tiger shrimp. Serve over steamed jasmine rice, which will soak up all the delicious juices.

3   pounds (1.4 kg) medium mild white or pink shrimp, preferably in the shell and head-on
¼   cup (60 ml) vegetable oil
3   large shallots, chopped
3   cloves garlic, chopped
2   stalks lemongrass, inner layers finely minced
1   cup (235 ml) dry white wine
¼   cup (62 g) Thai Green Curry Paste (page 49)

1   can (13.5 ounces, or 378 g) rich unsweetened coconut cream, preferably Thai
¼   cup (20 g) grated fresh coconut or shredded unsweetened coconut
1   small handful Thai basil, leaves shredded
    Jasmine rice, for serving

1. Devein the shrimp if desired—this is not usually necessary if the shrimp are smaller—leaving the last tail shell section on.

2. Heat the oil over medium heat in a large skillet, preferably nonstick. Add the shrimp and cook for about 2 minutes, or until partially opaque. Add the shallots, garlic, and lemongrass and sauté for about 1 minute, or until the shrimp are just cooked through and lightly curled up. Remove the shrimp from the pan and reserve. Add the wine to the skillet and cook over high heat until the liquid has mostly cooked away.

3. Add the Thai Green Curry Paste, coconut cream, and shredded coconut. Bring the mixture to a boil, and cook over moderately high heat until thickened enough for bubbles to appear all over the surface, about 3 minutes. Just before serving, return the shrimp to the pan, toss to combine with the sauce, and add the Thai basil. Serve immediately over rice.

YIELD: 6 servings

LATIN-AMERICAN
BLENDS

The five species of chile, *Capsicum frutescens, C. chinense, C. baccatum, C. pubescens,* and *C. annuum,* which may have originated in the Amazon, altered the cuisines of Africa, India, Southeast Asia, Latin America, and the Caribbean in fiery African spice blends, Indian masalas, and Southeast Asian curry pastes. The most famed spice blends are the colorful moles of Puebla and Oaxoca, Mexico.

Allspice was introduced to Europe from the Caribbean islands and is essential to Jamaica's jerk spice blend. Grenada raises 20 percent of the world's nutmeg, while Guatemala is a major exporter of cardamom. Pungent epazote and sweetly fragrant vanilla beans are indigenous to Mexico, while pink peppercorns and lemon verbena are native to South America. Deep red annatto, the base of Yucatán's Achiote Paste, is mainly produced in Peru and Brazil.

Dark red annatto seeds come from a tropical evergreen tree native to Latin America. They are used mainly for the intense red-orange color they impart to food. Look for the brightest, lipstick-red ground annatto, as the color varies greatly among brands. The whole seeds may be used but they are quite hard and must be crushed with a hammer or mallet.

Mexican oregano is a close relative of lemon verbena, with an intense but lemony aroma of oregano with a hint of licorice sweetness. It is preferred in Mexico over the more resinous, slightly harsh Mediterranean oregano.

YUCATÁN

ACHIOTE PASTE

This thick, deep red seasoning paste, also known as *recado colorado*, originated in the Yucatán, Mexico. It is best rubbed on chicken, pork, fish, or seafood, to which it imparts a deep red color and warm, mild flavor. Achiote paste is also sold in blocks ready to be mixed with bitter orange juice, a mixture of orange and lime juice, or mild vinegar. Bitter orange juice comes from bigarade, or Seville oranges, the same type of oranges used to make marmalade. It is grown throughout the Mediterranean and is common in Cuban and Latin-American cooking. The fresh fruit may occasionally be found in specialty markets in its winter season.

- 1 head (12 to 16 large cloves) garlic
- 3 tablespoons (15 g) coriander seeds
- 2 tablespoons (20 g) cumin seeds
- 1 tablespoon (8 g) black peppercorns
- 2 teaspoons (6 g) allspice berries
- 1 teaspoon whole cloves

- 1 cup (235 ml) bitter orange juice, or ¾ cup (180 ml) orange juice and ¼ cup (60 ml) lime juice
- 1 tablespoon (18 g) sea salt
- 3 tablespoons (30 g) ground annatto
- 1 tablespoon (2 g) dried Mexican or Mediterranean oregano

Peel off the outer layers of skin from the garlic. Separate into individual cloves with their skin on. Heat a dry skillet over medium heat and add the garlic. Roast until lightly charred, remove from the skillet, cool, and then peel. Add the coriander seeds, cumin seeds, peppercorns, allspice, and cloves to the same skillet. Toast lightly, shaking the skillet, until fragrant, about 3 minutes. Cool the spices to room temperature and then grind in a spice grinder or crush using a mortar and pestle. Combine the charred garlic, spices, orange juice, salt, and annatto in a food processor. Process to make a thick, wet paste. Transfer to a glass jar and store, refrigerated, for up to 2 months or freeze for up to 6 months.

YIELD: About 1½ cups (450 g)

QUESADILLAS WITH CHICKEN ADOBO, TOMATILLOS, AND GOUDA

Achiote Paste flavors and tenderizes the chicken in this dish and imparts its warm red color. Chicken thigh is preferable because it will stay moist even when cooked over high heat. This is one place where it's especially important to spring for high-quality, grain-fed, pastured or free-range chicken, as the fat contained in the thighs picks up off flavors from fish meal and growth hormones used to get commercial chickens to gain weight quickly. The chicken may be made separately several days ahead of time and then assembled and topped with the tomatillo salsa.

LATIN-AMERICAN BLENDS **55**

FOR CHICKEN ADOBO

¼ cup (75 g) Achiote Paste
2 tablespoons (30 ml) olive oil
2 tablespoons (30 ml) cider vinegar
1 teaspoon dried oregano
1 teaspoon sea salt
1 pound (454 g) boneless, skinless chicken thighs

FOR SALSA

2 firm, ripe tomatoes, diced
2 tomatillos, diced
½ sweet onion, diced
1 serrano chile, thinly sliced
1 lime, juiced
¼ cup (4 g) chopped cilantro
1 teaspoon kosher salt

FOR QUESADILLAS

4 ounces (112 g) Gouda, Chihuahua, or Monterey Jack cheese, shredded
8 to 10 corn tortillas, (6 inches, or 15 cm)
1 to 2 tablespoons (15 to 30 ml) canola oil, for griddle
¼ cup (60 ml) Mexican crema or sour cream
½ cup (65 g) pumpkin seeds (pepitas)

TO MAKE THE CHICKEN ADOBO:

1. Blend together the achiote, oil, vinegar, oregano, and salt in a large bowl. Add the chicken, turn to coat, cover with plastic, and refrigerate for 24 to 48 hours.
2. When ready to cook the chicken, preheat a grill and grill over indirect heat until the chicken is opaque and thoroughly cooked. Or preheat the oven 425°F (220°C, or gas mark 7) and roast for about 35 minutes, or broil under high heat, turning once, for about 20 minutes, until the chicken is opaque. Cool and then shred the chicken.

TO MAKE THE SALSA:

Combine the tomatoes, tomatillos, onion, chile, lime juice, cilantro, and salt in a bowl and set aside.

TO MAKE THE QUESADILLAS:

1. Preheat the oven to 350°F (180°C, or gas mark 4).
2. Place a portion of shredded cheese on one half of each tortilla. Top with a portion of chicken and sprinkle with more cheese. Fold over and press closed to form a half-moon shape. Preheat a cast-iron griddle or skillet, cover with a thin layer of oil, and heat until just starting to smoke.
3. Cook the quesadillas on both sides on the griddle until lightly charred, then transfer to a metal baking pan. Bake just long enough to melt the cheese, about 8 minutes. Top with the reserved salsa and dollops of crema and sprinkle with the pumpkin seeds. Serve immediately.

YIELD: 8 to 10 servings

MOLE

Mole is a group of complex Mexican sauces combining twenty-five or more spices and other ingredients from the Old and New Worlds. Because of this, many companies in Mexico, especially Oaxaca—mole central—make and pack the sauce for sale in glass jars. Mole comes in many versions, including mole amarillo (yellow mole), mole verde (green mole), mole poblano (from Puebla), and mole negro (black mole) from Oaxaca. All include at least one type of chile, often ancho, pasilla, mulato, or chipotle.

Other ingredients include sweet spices such as cinnamon from Sri Lanka and allspice from Jamaica; seeds and nuts such as almond and sesame from the Old World and peanuts and pumpkin seeds from the New World; sweet dried fruits (e.g. raisins and prunes) from the Old World; aromatic vegetables such as onion and garlic from sthe Old World; and tomato and tomatillo from the New World. Old World herbs (e.g. cilantro and parsley), New World herbs (e.g. hoja santa and epazote), starchy New World thickeners (e.g. plantain and corn masa), and even unsweetened chocolate.

The many ingredients are roasted and ground into a paste using a stone *molcajete* (mortar), a labor-intensive job that in the past involved multiple generations of women in a family when everything was done by hand. Today, while still challenging to make, the work goes much faster with the help of a *licuadora* (blender)—standard in many Mexican kitchens. Families often have their own recipe for mole that is prepared in large quantities for celebrations and holidays. Mole poblano is traditionally served with turkey, while other moles are served with chicken or pork.

SPICEMASTER'S NOTE

The palm-size, deep-veined velvety leaves of hoja santa *Piper sanctum* come from the peppercorn family and grow abundantly in south-central Mexico.

To make an authentic mole negro, stem, seed, and devein the chiles, reserving the seeds. Prepare the chile flesh as directed in the recipe, page 58. Preheat a heavy cast-iron skillet, until smoking. Add the seeds and toast in the skillet until charred deep brown. Avoid breathing the smoke. Cool, then grind to a fine powder, avoiding breathing the fumes, and blend with the finished sauce.

MOLE NEGRO

Charring all parts of the chile, including the seeds and ribs, gives this deep, dark spice sauce its characteristic, almost black color, but should only be attempted in a kitchen with really good ventilation. It's a good idea to wear a painter's mask to keep from breathing the strong fumes. The anise-like flavor of hoja santa leaves, is essential to its authentic flavor, but we have used more aniseed as a substitute.

OTHER SUGGESTED USES

Make extra of the toasted dry spice mix above (cinnamon, aniseed, cumin, peppercorns, and allspice) and use to season pork roast, turkey, squash, or sweet potatoes.

Use extra sauce to flavor the filling for tamales using cornhusk or banana leaf wrappings.

Add mole sauce to the filling for enchiladas, called enmoladas.

Serve Mole Negro over eggs.

4   ounces (112 g) dried guajillo chiles
4   ounces (112 g) dried mulato negro chiles
½   cup (2 ounces, or 56 g) blanched almonds
½   cup (2 ounces, or 56 g) sesame seeds
1   section (2 inches, or 5 cm) canela (true cinnamon), crushed
2   tablespoons (15 g) aniseed
1   tablespoon (10 g) cumin seeds
2   teaspoons (6 g) black peppercorns
2   teaspoons (6 g) whole allspice
1   teaspoon whole cloves
½   cup lard, bacon fat, or duck fat (112 g) or vegetable oil (120 ml), divided

2   stale corn tortillas, roughly chopped
1   small white onion, diced
4   large cloves garlic, chopped
3   ounces (84 g) roasted peanuts
½   cup (3 ounces, or 84 g) prunes
2   ounces (scant ½ cup, or 75 g) dark raisins
2   hoja santa leaves (see Spicemaster's Note) or 1 tablespoon (7.5 g) more aniseed (if using more aniseed, add with the prior aniseed)
1   tablespoon (18 g) sea salt
1   small very ripe plantain, cut into smaller pieces
4   ounces (112 g) unsweetened (baker's) chocolate, chopped

1. Remove the stems, seeds, and ribs from the chiles. Reserve the seeds if desired (see Spicemaster's Note, page 57). Place the flesh in a bowl with warm water to cover and soak for 30 minutes, or until soft and pliable. Reserve the soaking liquid.

2. Meanwhile, preheat the oven to 325°F (170°C, or gas mark 3). Spread the almonds and sesame seeds on a baking tray and roast until medium brown, about 15 minutes. Remove from the oven, cool, and reserve.

3. Heat a small skillet over medium heat. Add the cinnamon, aniseed, cumin, peppercorns, allspice, and cloves. Toast until brown and fragrant, about 3 minutes. Cool to room temperature. Grind in a spice grinder or mortar and pestle. Reserve.

4. In a medium skillet over medium heat, heat 2 tablespoons (28 g) of the lard and brown the tortillas until deep brown. Remove from the pan and reserve. Add 2 tablespoons (28 g) more lard to the pan and cook the onions until deep golden brown but not at all burned and bitter. Add the garlic, stir to combine, and cook until the garlic is fragrant, about 2 minutes longer. Turn off the heat and reserve.

5. Combine the soaked chiles, peanuts, almonds, sesame seeds, ground spices, onion mix, prunes, raisins, hoja santa, salt, and plantain in the jar of a blender and process to a thick, smooth paste, adding the chile soaking liquid to blend.

6. Transfer the resulting spice paste to a large, heavy Dutch oven along with the remaining ¼ cup (56 g) lard. Fry the paste over medium heat until it is thick enough to hold its shape and the fat rises to the surface, about 20 minutes, noting that it will spatter. Stir in the chocolate and remove from the heat. Stir in powder from reserved seeds, if using.

7. Cool the mole. Transfer to an airtight container. Refrigerate up to 3 months or freeze.

YIELD: About 2 quarts (1.8 kg)

TURKEY THIGHS IN OAXACAN MOLE NEGRO

The word *mole* comes from the Nahuatl word *molli*, meaning "concoction" or "mixture,"
and that it certainly is with all the many ingredients from both the Old World and the New.
There are strong Spanish influences in this dish with the use of almonds and sesame seeds
to thicken the sauce. Exotic spices such as true cinnamon, aniseed, cumin seeds, black
peppercorns, and cloves were brought by the Arabs to Spain; the Spanish, in turn, carried
them to Mexico. The allspice is native to the New World in Jamaica.

Moist, dark, richly flavored meat from the thighs of the turkey, a bird native to Mexico, where its name is *guajolote*, is put to excellent use here. Turkey thighs range in size and weight from about ½ pound (227 g) to more than 2 pounds (908 g) each, so adjust the cooking times accordingly.

2 **quarts (2 L) turkey or chicken stock**
1 **tablespoon (18 g) kosher salt**
2 **bay leaves**
5 **pounds (2.3 kg) bone-in turkey thighs (3 or 4 medium)**

2 **cups (450 g) mole negro (page 58)**
½ **cup (70 g) pumpkin seeds, for garnish**
  Cooked posole or rice, for serving

1. Bring the stock, salt, and bay leaves to a boil in a large pot over high heat. Add the turkey thighs, return to the boil, and then reduce the heat to a bare simmer. Cook until the meat is tender when pierced, about 1 hour, and then remove the pot from the heat. Allow the thighs to cool for about 30 minutes and then remove from the pot, reserving the liquid. Remove and discard the turkey skin and bones (or use to make another batch of turkey stock). Cut the turkey meat into bite-size chunks.

2. Preheat the oven to 325°F (170°C, or gas mark 3). Strain 1 cup (235 ml) of the poaching liquid (save the remainder for another use, such as soup or turkey gravy) and combine with the mole and cut-up turkey in an ovenproof casserole. Cover and bake for 1 hour, or until the turkey is fork-tender.

3. Sprinkle with the pumpkin seeds just before serving, accompanied by cooked posole or rice.

YIELD: 8 servings

MOLE VERDE

Tart and tangy green tomatillos, also known as *husk tomatoes*, are closely related to the ground cherries that grow abundantly in Pennsylvania. They are essential for this sauce. Like many Spanish sauces, this green mole is thickened with nuts or seeds—here, green pumpkin seeds, native to the New World. The technique of frying a sauce in lard is typical of Mexican cooking. The green herb purée added at the end of cooking brightens the color, a technique also used in French cooking.

½ pound (227 g) green pumpkin seeds
2 tablespoons (16 g) sesame seeds
2 teaspoons (6 g) cumin seeds
1 teaspoon black peppercorns
1 teaspoon whole allspice
1 section (2 inches, or 5 cm) true cinnamon quill, crushed
4 whole cloves
¼ cup lard (56 g) or olive oil (60 ml), divided
1 small white onion, roughly chopped
4 large cloves garlic, roughly chopped
1 pound (454 g) tomatillos, husk removed, quartered

2 green serrano chiles, trimmed and seeded
1 green poblano chile, trimmed and seeded
1 cup (235 ml) chicken or vegetable stock
1 handful baby spinach leaves
1 handful cilantro sprigs
1 handful Italian parsley sprigs
2 sprigs fresh epazote or 1 tablespoon (3 g) dried epazote (optional)
1 tablespoon (18 g) fine sea salt

1. Heat a large heavy skillet, preferably cast iron, over medium heat and toast the pumpkin seeds, stirring constantly, until they have puffed up and begin to pop, 3 to 5 minutes. Remove from the heat, cool to room temperature, and reserve.

2. In the same skillet, toast the sesame seeds, cumin seeds, peppercorns, allspice, cinnamon, and cloves, shaking the pan often, until lightly browned and fragrant, about 2 minutes. Remove from the heat and cool to room temperature, then grind to a fine powder in a spice grinder, blender, or mortar and pestle.

3. In the same skillet, heat 2 tablespoons (28 g) of the lard and cook the onion and garlic until softened, then add the tomatillos and both kinds of chiles and cook until soft and the sauce has thickened, about 10 minutes.

4. Combine the pumpkin seeds, ground spices, onion mix, and chicken stock in the jar of a blender and blend to a smooth paste. Scrape out the mixture, transfer to the skillet, and add the remaining 2 tablespoons (28 g) lard. Cook over low heat until the sauce has thickened, stirring frequently, about 20 minutes. Note that the sauce will splatter, so cook over low heat.

5. Meanwhile, place the spinach, cilantro, parsley, and epazote leaves in the blender and blend to a smooth paste, adding enough cold water to blend as needed.

6. Combine the herb purée with the cooked sauce to make a bright green mole verde. Season with salt and reserve. Reblend for a smoother sauce.

YIELD: About 6 cups (1.4 kg)

▶ DID YOU KNOW?

Eighty percent of Sri Lanka's exports of true cinnamon go to Mexico, where its floral scent and subtle, adaptable flavor is essential to blending complex moles and adobos.

OTHER SUGGESTED USES

Spoon dollops onto tortilla chips, top with queso anejo (or another white crumbling cheese such as feta), and bake.

Spoon onto grilled chicken breasts.

Spoon onto grilled fish.

Use as a sauce for chicken or cheese enchiladas.

POLLO EN MOLE VERDE

The classic combination combines lighter green herbal mole verde with chicken. Chicken thighs are moist and full of flavor, but it's important to purchase top-quality grain-fed or pastured chicken, which will have thighs that are milder in flavor. Because the thighs are fattier, they pick up off flavors easily. Low-priced commercial chicken is often fed with fish meal so the birds put on weight quickly—this "fishy" flavor transfers to the meat. If you prefer chicken breasts, poach them, but be extra careful not to overcook them, as white meat can get dry.

3 cups (705 ml) chicken stock
3 pounds (1.4 kg) chicken thighs on the bone

2 cups (450 g) Mole Verde (page 61)
Salt

1. Heat the chicken stock to a simmer in a wide, shallow pot. Add the chicken thighs and poach over low heat until the chicken is tender, about 20 minutes, turning the chicken over once so it cooks evenly. Remove the chicken from the liquid and pull off and discard the skin. Pour off and reserve the cooking liquid.

2. Place the cooked chicken back into the pot and spoon the Mole Verde on top. Cook over low heat until the sauce is bubbling hot, adding a little of the chicken poaching liquid as needed to make a thick but pourable and creamy sauce. Season with salt.

3. Serve immediately with tortillas, posole (hominy), or rice.

YIELD: 6 servings

TEMPERO BAIANO

This hot and spicy Brazilian seasoning blend comes from the African-influenced province of Bahia, famed for its bold, complex cuisine incorporating West African elements such as black-eyed peas, dende (palm) oil, peanuts, piri piri peppers, and dried shrimp. Every Brazilian kitchen (every cook, really) has its own interpretation, but most versions include white pepper, oregano, parsley, and various chiles. Some versions contain turmeric, nutmeg, and cumin, while others are more herbal and might also include marjoram, Mexican oregano, basil, and bay leaves.

- ¼ cup (24 g) ground cumin
- 2 tablespoons (12 g) ground coriander
- 2 tablespoons (20 g) ground turmeric
- 2 tablespoons (12 g) ground white pepper
- 1 tablespoon (8 g) ground piri piri or cayenne pepper
- ¼ cup (8 g) dried oregano

Combine all the ingredients in a small bowl and transfer to a tightly sealed storage container. Store in a cool, dark place for up to 3 months.

YIELD: About 1 cup (175 g)

BRAZILIAN BLACK BEAN FEIJOADA

The national dish of Brazil, feijoada is a humble dish of black beans cooked with and accompanied by smoked and cured meats. Because it is so filling and substantial, feijoada is eaten on Saturday afternoon, when there's plenty of time afterward for a long nap. We season the feijoada (which simply means "bean dish") with Tempero Baiano. Feijoada originated with African slave cooks who made creative use of collagen-rich pig ears, snouts, and tails, parts discarded by wealthy plantation owners. Here we serve the beans with smoked turkey, spiced and smoked pork spareribs, and Portuguese chouriço sausage. Start 3 or 4 days ahead of time to cure the meat. Garnish the platter with orange slices, rice, and wilted kale and accompany with molho (Brazilian chile-vinegar hot sauce). The final touch is a sprinkling of farofa, crunchy toasted meal made from ground, dried cassava or manioc root, which is native to Brazil.

FOR MEAT
- ½ cup (160 g) molasses (not blackstrap)
- 1 section (3 inches, or 7.5 cm) ginger root, peeled and roughly chopped
- ¼ cup (44 g) Tempero Baiano
- 8 large cloves garlic, roughly chopped
- 3 tablespoons (54 g) kosher salt
- 2 bone-in pork sparerib roasts (2 to 2½-pounds, or 908 g to 1 kg, each)

OTHER SUGGESTED USES

Use to season bean soups and hearty stews.

Add to fish and seafood ceviche.

Add to the batter for corn bread.

Rub bone-in, skin-on chicken thighs with the mixture and roast at a high temperature to brown.

FOR BEANS

- 2 pounds (908 g) smoked turkey wings, drumsticks, or thighs
- 6 bay leaves
- 1 white onion, peeled and quartered with root end attached
- 4 sprigs thyme, tied in kitchen string
- 1 gallon (3.6 L) cold water
- 2 pounds (908 g) dried black turtle beans, soaked in cold water to cover overnight
- 2 large white onions, diced
- 6 large cloves garlic, minced
- ¼ cup (26 g) Tempero Baiano (page 63)
- 2 tablespoons (12 g) ground cumin
- ½ cup (112 g) bacon fat
- 1 can (28 ounces, or 784 g) chopped plum tomatoes
- ½ cup (120 ml) malt vinegar
- 2 tablespoons (4 g) oregano
- 1 tablespoon (18 g) sea salt
- 2 pounds (908 g) Portuguese chouriço sausage, cut into ¾-inch (2 cm) diagonal slices
- 1 cup (150 g) farofa (optional), for garnish

TO MAKE THE MEAT:

1. Combine the molasses, ginger, Tempero Baiano, garlic, and salt in a blender or food processor and process into a paste. Rub all over the surface of the pork. Cover and refrigerate for 3 days to cure.

2. Wipe off the excess paste and hot-smoke according to your smoker manufacturer's directions for 4 hours, or until tender when pierced with a skewer and well browned. Or roast at 275°F (140°C, or gas mark 1) for 3 to 4 hours, or until the meat is tender when pierced with a skewer. Keep warm or reheat as necessary.

TO MAKE THE BEANS:

1. In a large soup pot, place the smoked turkey, bay leaves, onion quarters, thyme, and water. Bring to a boil, reduce the heat, and simmer for 2 hours, or until the broth is well flavored.

2. Drain and rinse the black beans. Add them to the pot and bring back to the boil. Skim off and discard the white scum that rises to the top. Simmer the beans until tender but not mushy, about 1½ hours. Remove and cool the turkey. Drain the beans, reserving any excess liquid for soup stock if desired. Pull the turkey meat off the bones, making sure to remove and discard the hard, bony tendons if using turkey drumsticks. Cut the meat into bite-size pieces and mix back into the beans.

3. Preheat the oven to 300°F (150°C, or gas mark 2).

4. In a large, heavy Dutch oven with a lid, sauté the diced onion, garlic, Tempero Baiano, and cumin in the bacon fat until softened but not browned. Stir in the tomatoes, vinegar, oregano, and salt, and bring to a boil. Stir in the cooked beans and reserved turkey meat and bring back to the boil. Cover and transfer to the oven. Bake for 1½ hours, or until the beans are soft and plump and most of the liquid has been absorbed.

5. To serve, cut the meat off the bones of the sparerib roast and slice or pull or dice into bite-size pieces. Brown the chouriço slices in a large skillet. Arrange the beans in the center of a large platter and place the chopped spareribs on one side of the beans and the chouriço on the other. Accompany with any or all of the garnishes listed in the headnote.

YIELD: 12 to 16 servings

ADOBO SEASONING

A fundamental seasoning in Spanish and Latin American cultures, adobo developed to preserve meats in the days before refrigeration. It gets its name from the Spanish word *adobar*, meaning "to marinate." Adobo can refer to either a wet paste of spices mixed with vinegar, bitter orange juice, or lemon or lime juice for acidity and olive or other oils for moisture, similar to Achiote Paste (page 54), which is a Yucatán adobo, or to a dry seasoning mixture, as in this recipe. Commercial adobo seasoning is quite common but is often laden with MSG. In the Philippines, a Spanish colony for close to four hundred years, the local version of adobo includes Chinese soy. Cuban adobo, with a strong Spanish influence, usually includes bitter (Seville) orange juice, cumin, and garlic, while Puerto Rican adobo includes vinegar and oregano.

6　tablespoons (36 g) freshly ground black pepper (use a spice grinder)
¾　cup (96 g) sweet paprika
6　tablespoons (42 g) onion powder
¼　cup (24 g) ground cumin
¼　cup (12 g) dried oregano

3　tablespoons (30 g) ground or crushed chipotle chile or other hot smoked pepper, such as picante Spanish pimentón
2　tablespoons (18 g) garlic powder

Combine all the ingredients and transfer to a tightly sealed storage container. Store in a cool, dark place for up to 3 months.

YIELD: About 2½ cups (200 g)

OTHER SUGGESTED USES

Rub generously on chicken, turkey, or pork before roasting at a high temperature.

Toss with roasted potatoes or plantains.

Use adobo to season guacamole, tacos, chili meat, or beans.

Rub on roasted or buttered steamed corn on the cob.

HONEY ADOBO-ROASTED SWEET POTATO WEDGES

Whether you call them yams, sweet potatoes, or sweetpotatoes (botanists prefer the last), these sweet, firm tubers take well to roasting, especially dense, nutty Mid-Atlantic U.S. heirloom white or yellow sweet potato varieties such as Hayman White or Jersey Yellow. Seasoning them first with mellow spiced adobo and a bit of honey turns a staple into a memorable side dish. Roast at high heat to caramelize the honey and the natural sugars in the yams and toast the spices, enhancing their flavor, but keep a careful eye so the yams don't burn.

2　pounds (908 g) sweet potatoes, peeled or not, as desired
¼　cup (80 g) honey
3　tablespoons (45 ml) vegetable oil

3　tablespoons (15 g) Adobo Seasoning
1　orange, zested
1　tablespoon (18 g) kosher salt

Preheat the oven to 375°F (190°C, or gas mark 5). Cut the sweet potatoes into thick wedges. Combine the honey, oil, adobo, orange zest, and salt in a small bowl. Rub generously over the sweet potato wedges. Arrange the sweet potatoes in a single layer in a baking dish. Roast for 30 to 40 minutes, or until the coating is browned and the sweet potatoes are tender at their thickest point. Serve immediately.

YIELD: 4 to 6 servings

POUDRE DE COLOMBO

Poudre de Colombo ("Colombo powder") originated with Sri Lankans who arrived in the French Caribbean islands of Martinique and Guadeloupe during the colonial era as indentured sugar plantation worker after the abolishment of slavery. Also known as Trinidad curry. *Colombo* is now a general term in the Caribbean for a curried meat or seafood stew, often made with goat meat and dense root vegetables like *boniato* and hard squash like calabaza. The toasted rice is typical of Colombo powder and helps bind the spices and lend a nutty, roasted flavor to the mix, which is relatively mild in flavor because it doesn't include chiles.

¼ cup (46 g) long-grain white rice
½ cup (80 g) cumin seeds
½ cup (40 g) coriander seeds
2 tablespoons (22 g) black mustard seeds

2 tablespoons (16 g) black peppercorns
2 tablespoons (25 g) fenugreek seeds
2 teaspoons (3 g) whole cloves
¼ cup (40 g) ground turmeric

1. Toast the rice in a dry, skillet over medium heat, shaking often, until light brown and fragrant, 3 to 4 minutes. Remove from the pan and cool to room temperature.
2. In the same skillet, toast the cumin seeds, coriander seeds, mustard seeds, black peppercorns, fenugreek, and cloves, shaking frequently, until lightly toasted and fragrant, about 2 to 3 minutes.
3. Cool the spices to room temperature and combine with the toasted rice. Grind to a fine powder and combine well with the turmeric. Transfer to a storage container and store in a cool, dark place for up to 4 months.

YIELD: About 2¼ cups (338 g)

OTHER SUGGESTED USES

Add to Caribbean-style beef, lamb, goat, or chicken stew.

Use to season hard winter squash such as butternut, calabaza, or pumpkin.

Sprinkle on buttered popcorn.

Add to the filling for deviled eggs.

CARROT-GINGER BISQUE WITH POUDRE DE COLOMBO

This cheerful, sunny yellow-orange soup can be made easily with found pantry ingredients and carrots. Infused with the flavors of poudre de Colombo and enriched with coconut milk, the soup is also suitable for vegans. A generous quantity of sweet-hot fresh ginger adds sparkle, while the toasted coconut garnish provides a bit of crunch.

¼ cup (60 ml) vegetable oil
2 ribs celery, diced
1 large onion, diced
3 pounds (1.4 kg) carrots, peeled and roughly chopped
3 cloves garlic, minced
1 section (3 inches, or 7.5 cm) fresh gingerroot, peeled, sliced, and chopped
¼ cup (46 g) long-grain white rice

1½ cups (107 g) dried unsweetened coconut, divided
¼ cup (38 g) poudre de Colombo
3 quarts (2.7 L) vegetable stock, homemade or store-bought, simmering
3 cans (14.5 ounces, or 406 g each) unsweetened coconut milk
¼ cup (80 g) honey
Sea salt and freshly ground black pepper

1. Heat the oil with the celery, onion, carrots, garlic, and ginger in a large soup pot and cook over medium heat until the vegetables are soft but not at all brown. Add the rice and ½ cup (22 g) of the coconut and cook until translucent, about 3 minutes. Add the Poudre de Colombo and continue to cook until fragrant, about 2 minutes, stirring constantly.

2. Add the vegetable stock and bring to a boil. Reduce the heat to a simmer and cook until the carrots are quite soft, about 30 minutes. Add the coconut milk and honey, bring back to the boil, and remove from the heat. Season with salt and pepper.

3. Preheat the oven to 325°F (170°C, or gas mark 3).

4. Meanwhile, spread the remaining 1 cup (85 g) coconut in a thin layer on a baking pan. Place in the oven and toast until lightly and evenly browned, about 12 minutes, stirring once or twice.

5. Working in batches, blend the soup to a smooth purée in a blender or using an immersion blender. Serve immediately, garnished with the toasted coconut.

6. To store, cool the soup to room temperature, then transfer to a storage container. Store refrigerated for up to 5 days or freeze for up to 3 months.

YIELD: 10 to 12 servings

JERK SEASONING

This fiery and aromatic spice paste from Jamaica is used to marinate chicken and pork for Caribbean-style barbecue. It is based on Jamaican allspice berries (known there as pimento), mellow cinnamon, resinous thyme, and Scotch bonnet peppers, which we add in fresh form to the marinade for the turkey wings. Similar lantern-shaped habanero chiles also impart the raisin-like fruity-fiery flavor of Caribbean chiles. Jamaica was settled over 2,500 years ago by Arawak Indians from South America, where they smoked and dried meat in the sun or over a slow fire, methods that were common in Peru. Food historians tell us that the word *jerk* derives from the Peruvian word *charqui*, for the strips of smoke-dried meat that became known as jerky in America.

6 **tablespoons (48 g) whole allspice**	¼ **cup (60 g) packed dark brown sugar**
10 **bay leaves, crumbled**	2 **tablespoons (5 g) chopped fresh thyme leaves or 2 teaspoons (2 g) dried**
2 **large quills soft-stick cinnamon (canela)**	**Kosher salt**
2 **tablespoons (16 g) black peppercorns**	

Heat the allspice, bay leaves, cinnamon, and peppercorns in a small, dry skillet over medium heat, shaking the pan for several minutes, or until the fragrance is released. Cool to room temperature and then grind in a spice grinder or crush using a mortar and pestle. Combine with the brown sugar, thyme, and salt and reserve. Transfer to a tightly sealed storage container. Store in a cool, dark place for up to 3 months.

YIELD: About 1 cup (75 g)

JERK-SPICED TURKEY WINGS

Allspice is native to Jamaica, and all parts of the plant are used for seasoning. The berries are crushed and used to season meats; the fresh leaves (also known as West Indian bay leaf) are used to wrap meat before cooking. Jamaica dram is a liqueur made by steeping allspice berries. The tree wood is used to make the fire when cooking jerk meats. While Mexico and several countries in Central America now raise allspice, the best-quality berries still come from Jamaica.

5 **pounds (2,270 g) turkey wings, defrosted if frozen**	2 **Scotch bonnet or habanero chiles, seeded and minced (wear gloves and take care as these chiles are fiery)**
6 **tablespoons (30 g) Jerk Seasoning**	1 **bunch scallions, thinly sliced**
1½ **cups (355 ml) malt or cider vinegar**	¼ **cup (60 ml) vegetable oil**
3 **cups (705 ml) water**	

1. Cut the wings into individual joints and use only the larger second and third joints. Reserve the wing tips for stock if desired.

2. In a large, nonreactive bowl, combine the Jerk Seasoning, vinegar, water, chiles, scallions, and turkey wings. Cover and refrigerate for 24 to 48 hours (longer is better here), turning once or twice so the wings marinate evenly.

3. When ready to cook, allow the wings to come to room temperature, about 1 hour. Preheat a charcoal grill with a cover until no flames remain, just white coals. Drain the wings and rub or brush with the oil. Grill indirectly in a covered grill until browned to a reddish mahogany color on all sides and cooked through but still juicy, about 1 hour,

OTHER SUGGESTED USES

Rub on chicken wings and marinate overnight before slow-grilling.

Rub on pork loin or tenderloin, marinate overnight, and then slow-grill.

Rub on pineapple, papaya, and/or firm mango slices and grill.

15 minutes. If desired, toss a small handful of whole allspice berries and/or cinnamon sticks into the fire halfway through the cooking time for an extra burst of flavor. Alternatively, preheat the oven to 350°F (180°C, or gas mark 4) and roast the wings until thoroughly cooked, about 1 hour.

YIELD: 6 servings

EUROPEAN
BLENDS

The best known of the short list of native European spices are pungent caraway, celery, chives, horseradish, and juniper. Though rare and costly, tropical spices such as black pepper, cinnamon, and ginger have been imported to the region since ancient Roman times. Europe's cuisines rely on Mediterranean herbs, including bay leaf, marjoram, chervil, parsley, oregano, rosemary, savory, sorrel, and thyme. In their fresh form, they show up in French Fines Herbes and Bouquet Garni. In their dried form, they are blended into Herbes de Provence.

Georgia, at the crossroads of western Asia and Eastern Europe, combines many herbs in its Khmeli-Suneli blend. Onion and garlic are important, especially in France and Italy, though garlic is less appreciated in Northern Europe. Hungary is renowned for its sweet and hot paprika, which developed from imported New World chiles. Black pepper seasons almost every savory dish, while white pepper is preferred for French white sauces. Ginger, nutmeg, mace, cinnamon, and cloves are commonly found in blends such as Dutch Speculaas Spice, Northern European Gingerbread Spice, Pickling Spice, and French Quatre Épices.

BOUQUET GARNI

This French term refers to a small bundle of fragrant herbs to be simmered with various dishes, infusing mild, aromatic flavor into the food. It nearly always contains parsley, thyme, and bay leaf, but delicate, slightly licorice-like chervil is a wonderful addition, especially when cooking chicken, veal, or fish. In Germany and Italy, other variations are used and might include basil, salad burnet, rosemary, savory, and tarragon. The orange peel used here is a Provençal French addition.

6	large sprigs thyme, preferably French small-leafed thyme	6	sprigs chervil (if available)
4	sprigs Italian or curly parsley	1	strip orange peel
		2	bay leaves

Using kitchen string, tie together the herbs, placing the bay leaves in the center of the bundle and wrapping the string tightly around and around so the bouquet doesn't unravel. Leave a long string tail that you can fish the bouquet out of the pot before serving.

YIELD: 1 bouquet

OTHER SUGGESTED USES

Add to stocks, sauces, soup, ragouts, and braised meats from the French and Italian traditions.

Add to boiling water and simmer for 15 to 20 minutes before cooking vegetables.

ROOT VEGETABLE POTAGE

A potage is a simple, country-style French soup that might be served in a farmhouse. Here we combine buttery-tasting gold potatoes with root vegetables simmered in chicken stock and enriched with cream just before serving. Feel free to substitute other root vegetables such as salsify (delicious but hard to find), gold beets, or parsley root. The soup freezes perfectly without the cream.

3 tablespoons (42 g) unsalted butter
1 large onion, roughly chopped
1 large celery root, pared and cut into rough chunks
2 large parsnips, pared and cut into rough chunks
3 large carrots, peeled and cut into rough chunks
3 large gold potatoes, peeled and cut into rough chunks
1 Bouquet Garni (page 74)

3 quarts (2.7 L) chicken stock, simmering (substitute vegetable stock for a vegetarian soup)
2 leeks, white and light green portions only, diced and washed
1 cup (235 ml) heavy cream
Kosher salt, ground white pepper, a pinch of cayenne, and freshly grated nutmeg to taste
Thinly sliced chives, for garnish (optional but lovely)

1. In a large soup pot, melt the butter and cook the onion, celery root, parsnips, and carrots until softened but not browned. Add the potatoes and bouquet garni and cook until soft, about 15 minutes. Add the chicken stock and continue cooking for another 10 minutes, or until the flavors come together.

2. Fish out and discard the Bouquet Garni. Working in batches and taking care because the soup is hot, blend the soup to a smooth purée. Stir in the leeks, transfer back to the pot, and cook for 5 minutes, or until the leeks are brightly colored and crisp-tender. Pour in the heavy cream, stir to combine, and bring back to the boil. Season to taste with salt, pepper, cayenne, and nutmeg. Serve the soup immediately topped with the chives.

YIELD: 8 to 10 servings

FINES HERBES

This classic blend is a delicately balanced bouquet of the fresh tender herbs popular in French cuisine. Use Fines Herbes to season mildly flavored dishes such as omelets, fish, veal dishes, mashed potatoes, and steamed or sautéed vegetables. Here we use fresh herbs, for a mixture to be used immediately. For a longer-lasting mix, substitute dried herbs, preferably those you have dried yourself on the branch (see page 18), in the same proportions. While it's not easy to find, feathery chervil is essential to its flavor. French tarragon, rather than the more common Russian tarragon, has finer leaves and a more pungent, licorice-like flavor.

2 tablespoons (8 g) finely chopped Italian parsley
2 tablespoons (6 g) thinly sliced chives
2 tablespoons (5 g) finely chopped chervil
2 tablespoons (8 g) finely chopped tarragon
1 tablespoon (2.5 g) finely chopped thyme

Combine all the ingredients in a small bowl and use the same day. Or, use dried herbs in the same proportion and combine well.

YIELD: About ½ cup (25 g)

SMOKED SALMON SCONES WITH FRENCH FINES HERBES

Scones are simply biscuits shortened with plenty of butter and raised with baking powder—somewhere between a pastry and a cake. Here we make savory scones speckled with bits of fresh green herbs and strips of savory smoked salmon. The dough freezes quite well. Either freeze the extra dough in a tightly closed resealable plastic bag, or roll out and cut the scones, place on a parchment paper–lined baking sheet, freeze until firm, then transfer to a resealable plastic bag, squeeze out the excess air, and freeze. Bake scones directly from frozen, allowing about 10 minutes extra baking time. Low-protein pastry flour, made from soft wheat and available from specialty bakery suppliers, makes for the most tender and moist scones.

1¼ pounds (about 5 cups, or 568 g) pastry flour
2 tablespoons (28 g) baking powder
2 teaspoons (12 g) sea salt
6 tablespoons (30 g) fresh Fines Herbes or 2 tablespoons (30 g) dried
1 pinch of cayenne
¼ teaspoon ground black pepper
14 ounces (392 g) unsalted butter, diced and chilled
6 tablespoons (90 ml) buttermilk
4 ounces (112 g) smoked salmon, trimmed and cut into thin strips
2 ounces (¼ cup, or 56 g) unsalted butter, melted and cooled
   Crème fraîche, chives, and salmon or tobiko caviar, for garnish

1. In a large bowl, whisk together the flour, baking powder, salt, fines herbes (dry or fresh), cayenne, and black pepper. In hot weather, chill in the freezer for 30 minutes. Using the flat beater from an electric mixer, or by hand, cut the butter into the flour mixture until the butter pieces are the size of peas.

2. Pour the buttermilk over the flour mixture while tossing with your hands to distribute the liquid evenly. Add the smoked salmon and toss to combine well. Mix just long enough for the mixture to form a rough ball (overbeating will yield tough scones).

3. Form the dough into a flattened rectangular block and store in resealable plastic bag. Chill for at least 1 hour, or until firm.

4. Preheat the oven to 350°F (180°C, or gas mark 4). Line baking sheets with parchment paper.

5. Roll out the dough on a floured surface (or between two sheets of wax paper that have been dusted with flour) to a thickness of about ⅜ inch (1 cm). Cut into 2-inch (5 cm) circles and brush with the melted butter. Arrange the scones equidistant on the prepared baking sheets. If desired, gather dough scraps together, flatten, and roll out again.

6. Bake for 25 minutes, or until the scones are fully cooked on the inside and lightly colored on the outside. Serve immediately topped with a dab of crème fraîche and a sprinkle of chives and caviar.

YIELD: 48 scones, 3¼ pounds (1.5 kg) dough

HERBES DE PROVENCE

This blend of herbs is essential to Provençal French cuisine, although it wasn't until the 1970s that commercial versions came on the market. Up until then, locals made their own blends of the herbs that they gathered or grew and dried. It is based on the resinous herbs laden with essential oils that thrive on hillsides throughout Provence and is almost always made with herbs that are sun-dried each season on the branch.

- 1 orange, zested, or 2 teaspoons (4 g) dried orange zest
- ¼ cup (4 g) dried tarragon
- ¼ cup (24 g) dried thyme
- 2 tablespoons (15 g) dried summer savory
- 2 tablespoons (12 g) ground fennel seed
- 2 teaspoons (4 g) celery seed
- 4 bay leaves, finely crumbled
- 2 teaspoons (2 g) lavender buds
- 1 teaspoon ground white pepper

Combine all the ingredients in a small bowl. Store in a tightly sealed container in a dark place for up to 3 months.

YIELD: About 1 cup (60 g)

PROVENÇAL SUMMER VEGETABLE TIAN

A favorite in summertime, the classic Provençal tian is named after the shallow, oval earthenware baking dish used to bake it. It is equally delicious served hot or at room temperature. If the yellow squash are large, you may wish to cut away the outside from the lower, fatter portion, discarding the seedy center portion, which may be woody. Cut the top, portion into rounds; cut the outer portion of the bottom into half-moons.

- 2 large red peppers
- 1 pound (454 g) eggplant, preferably slender Chinese or Japanese eggplant
- 2 pounds (908 g) ripe beefsteak tomatoes
- 1 pound (454 g) zucchini
- 1 fennel bulb, tough outer leaves discarded
- 1 lemon, juiced
- ¾ cup (120 ml) extra-virgin olive oil, divided
- Sea salt and freshly ground black pepper
- 1 red onion, diced
- 2 tablespoons (20 g) finely chopped garlic, divided
- 2 cups (100 g) fresh breadcrumbs (made from the insides of French baguette or Italian country bread and processed)
- 2 tablespoons (8 g) Herbes de Provence

1. Preheat the oven to 350°F (180°C, or gas mark 4).

2. Trim the red pepper, eggplant, tomatoes, zucchini, and fennel into rounds of equal thickness, about ¼ inch (6 mm). Toss the fennel with the lemon juice to prevent browning. Toss the vegetables with ¼ cup (60 ml) olive oil and season with salt and pepper.

3. Combine ¼ cup (60 ml) of the olive oil, the onion, and 1 tablespoon (10 g) of the garlic in a skillet. Cook slowly until softened but not browned, about 5 minutes. Spread half the onion mixture on the bottom of a large, shallow ceramic baking dish, and season with salt and pepper.

OTHER SUGGESTED USES

Rub on shoulder of lamb and slow-roast.

Add to vegetable stews like ratatouille and baked-stuffed vegetables such as tomatoes, peppers, and zucchini.

Use to season fennel, eggplant, and artichoke dishes.

4. In a small bowl, mix the breadcrumbs, remaining ¼ cup (60 ml) olive oil, Herbes de Provence, remaining 1 tablespoon (10 g) garlic, and more salt and pepper. Spread half the sliced vegetables on top. Pat half the breadcrumb mixture over the vegetables. Spread the remaining onion mixture on top of the onion mixture. Make a second layer of the sliced vegetables and top with the remaining crumb mixture.

5. Place the tian on a baking pan to catch any drips and place on the bottom shelf of the oven, cover with foil, and bake for 1½ hours or until the vegetables are bubbling. Uncover and continue baking 30 minutes or until the crumbs are golden brown and the vegetables are soft. Serve immediately or at room temperature.

YIELD: 8 to 10 servings

QUATRE ÉPICES

The French four-spice mixture is a simple combination of white pepper and sweet aromatic spices that dates back to prerevolutionary France. Sometimes cloves are substituted for the allspice. If doing so, use 2 teaspoons (6 g) ground cloves, as they are quite potent. Cinnamon may be substituted for all or part of the ginger if desired. Though white pepper is traditional, black pepper may be substituted for all or half of the white pepper, which is more potent and earthier than the more aromatic and fruitier black pepper. It is the classic seasoning for charcuterie such as pâté, sausage, and terrines.

½ cup (48 g) freshly ground white pepper

¼ cup (32 g) freshly ground nutmeg

¼ cup (24 g) ground ginger

2 tablespoons (12 g) ground allspice

Combine all the ingredients in a small bowl. Store in a tightly sealed container away from the light for up to 3 months.

YIELD: About 1 cup (85 g)

WINTER BOSC PEAR AND ROQUEFORT SALAD WITH SPICED RED WINE FIGS

This elegant cold-weather salad is made with Bosc pears, which have a spicy quality of their own, tossed with refreshingly bitter Belgian endive and radicchio—botanical cousins. Choose either the high-ground-grown, long, smooth, pointy spears of radicchio di Treviso or the more common low-ground-grown rounded curly heads of radicchio di Chioggia. The salad is garnished with dried figs simmered in red wine and honey with French Quatre Épices to add depth and a sweet-spicy fragrance. The sharp, biting flavor and richly buttery texture of Roquefort cheese brings all the flavors and textures together.

12 dried figs, preferably plump, light-colored Calimyrna

1 cup (235 ml) dry red wine

¼ cup (80 g) honey

3 teaspoons (6 g) Quatre Épices, divided

6 tablespoons (90 ml) grapeseed oil or other neutral salad oil such as canola

3 tablespoons (45 ml) cider vinegar

2 tablespoons (20 g) finely chopped shallot

Kosher salt and freshly ground black pepper

3 heads Belgian endive

1 head radicchio

3 Bosc pears

½ lemon, juiced

6 ounces (168 g) Roquefort cheese, cut into 6 slices

1. Trim off and discard the stems from the figs. In a pan, heat the red wine, honey, and 2 teaspoons (4 g) of the Quatre Épices until hot to the touch, turn off the heat, and then add the figs. Allow the figs to soak in the wine syrup for 2 hours, or until softened. Transfer to a medium pot and heat the mixture until boiling. Reduce the heat to low and simmer for 15 minutes, or until soft but still whole. Cool completely, then cut each fig in half.

2. Whisk together the oil, vinegar, shallot, and remaining 1 teaspoon (2 g) Quatre Épices and season with salt and pepper; reserve.

OTHER SUGGESTED USES

Use to season French country pâtés and terrines.

Add to braised beef in red wine sauce with marrow.

Add to veal stew and braised chicken dishes.

3. Cut the endive and radicchio into 1-inch (2.5 cm)-wide strips, discarding the hard cores. Halve the pears, remove the core, preferably using a Parisienne scoop (small round ball cutter), cut into thin wedges, and toss with the lemon juice.

4. Place the endive and radicchio in a bowl and toss with enough vinaigrette to coat lightly. Divide among six salad plates. Form the pear slices into six fans and place on one side of the salad, drizzling with more vinaigrette. Place a slice of Roquefort along the front edge of each pear fan. Arrange the figs on top of each salad and serve immediately.

YIELD: 6 servings

KHMELI-SUNELI

Georgia is well known for the subtle blends of herbs in its khmeli-suneli, which is used liberally to flavor kharcho, a thick stew-like soup made from beef, lamb, or chicken. In Georgia and in Russian markets, the pale gold to light brown mix can be purchased ready-made. This savory mixture of dried herbs (marjoram, basil, savory, dill, and others) includes black pepper, coriander seeds, and Georgian or Imeretian saffron (marigold or safflower petals) for their gold color. Marigolds are used in chicken feed to give their eggs a golden color.

2 **tablespoons (6 g) dried dill weed**
2 **tablespoons (15 g) dried summer savory**
2 **tablespoons (3.5 g) dried marjoram**
2 **tablespoons (3 g) dried spearmint**
¼ **cup (5 g) dried parsley**
2 **tablespoons (12 g) ground coriander**

2 **tablespoons (5 g) dried fenugreek (methi) leaves**
2 **teaspoons (15 g) ground fenugreek**
2 **teaspoons (4 g) ground black pepper**
1 **teaspoon celery seed**
4 **finely crushed bay leaves**
2 **tablespoons (2 g) dried crumbled marigold petals**

Combine everything but the marigold petals in a bowl. Grind the mixture to a slightly chunky consistency. Add the marigold and mix to combine well. Transfer the mixture to a tightly sealed storage container. Store in a cool, dark place for up to 3 months.

YIELD: About 1 cup (80 g)

▶ DID YOU KNOW?

Twelve to 20 grams of saffron can cause death by poisoning, but don't worry; an average serving is a pinch, weighing far less than 1 gram.

SPICEMASTER'S NOTE

Dry your own marigold by tying the bunch and hanging upside down until the blossoms are fully dried. Crumble the golden petals only, not the calyxes or other parts. Or purchase marigold (*Calendula officinalis*) tea bags, which are often available in Chinese markets and online shopping sites, and add the golden petals (not the green calyxes or other parts) to the mixture.

LOBIO (GEORGIAN RED KIDNEY BEAN STEW)

Food is an integral part of Georgia's legendary hospitality, demonstrated in feasts called *supra*, where a huge assortment of dishes is served accompanied by copious amounts of wine. This juicy red bean stew flavored with sweet-tart prunes, tangy tamarind, and Khmeli-Suneli is perfect for vegetarians and will also appeal to meat eaters. Look for dark red kidney beans (called *badi rajma* in Indian groceries).

1 pound (2 cups, or 454 g) dried dark red kidney beans	8 plump pitted prunes
Sea salt	¼ cup (60 ml) red wine vinegar
6 tablespoons (90 ml) extra-virgin olive oil	¼ cup (75 g) tamarind purée (see Note)
1 large onion, finely diced	½ teaspoon hot pepper flakes
2 carrots, finely diced	¼ cup (20 g) khmeli-suneli (page 82)
2 ribs celery, finely diced	½ bunch cilantro, chopped
4 cloves garlic, minced	Freshly ground black pepper

1. Soak the beans overnight in cold water to cover. Drain the beans and rinse well.

2. Place the beans in a large Dutch oven with cold water to cover. Bring to a boil, skimming off white foam impurities as they form. Cover and simmer for about 1 hour, or until the beans are half cooked. Season with salt and continue cooking 1 hour longer, or until the beans are tender but not mushy. Drain and set aside.

3. In a skillet, heat the olive oil over medium heat. Add the onion, carrots, celery, and garlic; sauté until crisp-tender, about 5 minutes. Remove from the heat and reserve.

4. Combine the prunes, vinegar, tamarind purée, and hot pepper flakes in a small pot. Simmer until the prunes are soft, about 15 minutes. Cool and then purée the mixture in a food processor or blender.

5. Add the sautéed vegetables, prune mixture, Khmeli-Suneli, and cilantro to the beans heating until bubbling hot. Season with more salt and freshly ground pepper and serve.

YIELD: 8 servings

▶ TAMARIND PURÉE

Tamarind is a pod that grows on a tree native to tropical Africa but was introduced to India so long ago that it is often thought to be indigenous there as well. It is cultivated extensively throughout the tropical regions, especially Mexico, Asian tamarinds have longer pods with six to twelve seeds; African and Latin American tamarinds have shorter pods containing one to six seeds. The seeds are flattened and glossy brown, and their flavor is like a lemony prune. Tamarind paste in a jar is available but is quite salty, so reduce or eliminate the salt in the recipe. Fresh tamarind may be found in Asian and Latino groceries in season—sporadically from early spring to late fall. To use fresh tamarind, remove the brown seedy meat from inside the hard, lumpy pod or use a 12-ounce (336 g) block of dried tamarind, preferably without seeds.

Place the block of tamarind in a bowl and cover with hot water. Soak until softened, about 30 minutes, breaking up the pulp with your hands to speed the process. When the tamarind is soft, strain the mixture through a sieve or food mill, discarding the fibers and seeds. The strained tamarind liquid is ready to use. Store refrigerated for up to 1 month or freeze for up to 6 months. Makes about 3 cups (900 g).

OTHER SUGGESTED USES

Use to flavors Georgian braised mutton.

Add to *givetch* (slow-cooked vegetable stew).

Add to marinades for meat and poultry.

Sprinkle on white cheese such as feta, labne, or farmer cheese as a spread for bread or a dip for vegetables.

SPECULAAS SPICE

Known as *speculaaskruiden* in Dutch, this mixture of aromatic sweet spices is used to make decorative speculaas cookies formed in carved wooden molds and *gevulde speculaas*, an almond paste–stuffed pastry similar to French *pithiviers* tart. The mix is a legacy of Holland's long history of colonization in Indonesia, home to cassia cinnamon. It also includes nutmeg, mace, and cloves, other spices grown in the Moluccas, the island archipelago in Indonesia long known as the Spice Islands.

- 6 tablespoons (36 g) ground Indonesian (cassia) cinnamon
- 2 tablespoons (12 g) ground ginger
- 2 tablespoons (12 g) ground aniseed
- 4 teaspoons (8 g) ground coriander
- 1 tablespoon (6 g) ground cardamom
- 2 teaspoons (6 g) freshly grated nutmeg
- 2 teaspoons (4 g) ground allspice
- 2 teaspoons (4 g) ground mace
- 1 teaspoon ground cloves

Combine all the spices in a small bowl. Store in a spice tin or glass jar in a cool, dark place for up to 4 months.

YIELD: About 1 cup (90 g)

▶ DID YOU KNOW?

The tiny island of Grenada in the Caribbean supplies nearly 40 percent of the world's nutmeg, which was introduced there in 1843 when a merchant ship called in on its way to England from the East Indies and left a few nutmeg trees behind.

DUTCH APPLE CAKE WITH CURRANTS AND SPECULAAS SPICE

Made with a mixture of tart, sweet, soft, and firm apples and tiny zante currant grapes, enclosed in buttery-rich cookie-like pastry, this deep-dish tart gets its flavor from lemon zest and Speculaas Spice. Serve warm with hot tea or coffee on a cold winter's day, preferably while sitting in front of the fire.

OTHER SUGGESTED USES

Add to sugar cookie dough.

Add to pancake batter.

Add to baked apples, pears, or apricots.

FOR FILLING
- 5 pounds (2.3 kg) mixed tart and sweet apples
- 1 cup (235 ml) water
- 1½ cups (300 g) sugar
- 1 lemon, zested
- 2 teaspoons (4 g) Speculaas Spice
- ½ teaspoon sea salt
- ¼ cup (36 g) Zante currants

FOR DOUGH
- 12 ounces (336 g) unbleached all-purpose flour
- 8 ounces (227 g) unsalted butter, cut into small bits
- ½ cup (100 g) sugar
- 2 teaspoons (4 g) Speculaas Spice
- 1 teaspoon sea salt
- 2 large eggs, lightly beaten with 2 tablespoons (30 ml) ice water
- 1 large egg, lightly beaten with 1 tablespoon (15 ml) milk or cream (for egg wash)

TO MAKE THE FILLING:

1. Peel and slice the apples. Bring the water and sugar to a boil in a medium pot over medium-high heat. Stir in the lemon zest, speculaas spice, and salt. Add the apples and simmer until transparent, about 15 minutes. Remove from the heat and stir in the currants.

2. Drain, reserving the fruit and liquid separately. Spread the fruit out on a parchment paper–lined metal pan so it will cool more quickly.

TO MAKE THE DOUGH:

1. Combine the flour, butter, sugar, Speculaas Spice, and salt in a mixing bowl and refrigerate, about 20 minutes. Using the flat paddle of a mixer, or by hand, cut the butter into the flour, mixing until the bits resemble oatmeal. Add the egg-water mixture and beat until the dough comes together in a rough ball. Add more ice water by the teaspoon as needed but avoid adding excess water because this will yield a tougher dough.

2. Pat the dough into a flattened rectangle, place in a plastic bag, and chill for at least 1 hour or up to 2 days, until firm. Divide the dough into two sections of one-third and two-thirds. Roll out the larger portion of dough on a generously floured surface into a round a bit more than ¼ inch (6 mm) thick, and chill. Roll the remaining smaller portion of dough into a roughly rectangular shape and chill. Alternatively, or on a hot day, dust a sheet of wax or parchment paper generously with flour. Top with the flattened dough, dust with flour, and top with another sheet of paper. Roll the dough between the sheets, removing from the paper and dusting with more flour to keep this sticky dough rolling freely. If the dough gets too soft, place back in the refrigerator to firm up before proceeding.

3. From the larger round of chilled dough, cut out a round about 12 inches (30.5 cm) in diameter. Press the round of dough into the bottom and about 1½ inches (3.8 cm) up the sides of a 9 x 2-inch (23 x 5 cm) springform pan or a similarly sized deep French quiche pan with a removable bottom.

4. Cut the remaining rectangular sheet of dough into strips about ⅓ inch (8 mm) wide for the lattice top, using a pinked cutter if possible. Arrange the strips on a sheet of parchment or waxed paper. Chill the strips while assembling the cake.

5. Preheat the oven to 350°F (180°C, or gas mark 4). Fill the pastry-lined pan with the cooled apple/currant mixture.

6. Make a woven lattice top to cover the top as follows: Place the dough strips in parallel rows across the top of the cake about ¾ inch (2 cm) apart. Fold back every other strip halfway. Place a dough strip crosswise over the strips. Unfold the folded strips to cover the crosswise strip.

7. Next, take the parallel strips that are running underneath the crosswise strip and fold them back halfway. Lay down a second crosswise strip of dough above the first strip, leaving ¾ inch (2 cm) in between the strips. Continue until the lattice top is complete. Trim any overhanging edges flush with the edge of the pan and press the edges together to seal.

8. Using the remaining dough strips, form a continuous border about ⅓-inch (8 mm) wide around the rim of the cake, covering the edges of the lattice. Press down evenly and lightly so the strips adhere to the rim. Brush the lattice and the rim with the egg-milk wash.

9. Place the cake on a baking sheet to catch any drips and bake on the bottom shelf of the oven until the dough is lightly browned and the filling is bubbling, about 1 hour and 15 minutes. Remove the cake from the oven and cool for about 30 minutes, or until warm but not hot.

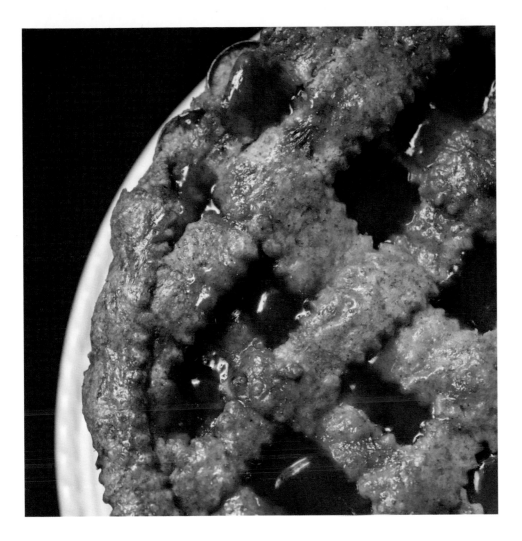

10. Meanwhile, boil the reserved apple syrup until thick and syrupy and just beginning to darken and then pour over the warm cake into the openings between the pastry strips. (Don't worry if some spills onto the pastry—this is expected.)

11. Cool the cake to room temperature before cutting into 12 to 16 wedges. Cover and store at room temperature for up to 1 day or refrigerate for up to 4 days.

YIELD: One 9-inch (23 cm) cake, 12 to 16 servings

GINGERBREAD SPICE MIX

Ginger is the dominant flavor in this sweet-hot aromatic spice mix and acts as a preservative to all manner of spiced gingerbreads. Whether soft and chewy, crisp and flat, or thick and breadlike, gingerbread has been baked in Europe, especially Germany, since the eleventh century. It was usually cut into shapes like men, women, children, animals, or stars or pressed into decorative molds before baking. The dough might be formed into the shape of a loved one, a heart shape decorated with white icing and colored ribbons, or used to construct elaborate iced and candy-laden gingerbread houses. Because of the costliness of the spices that arrived from far-off lands, gingerbread was reserved for Christmas and festivals. In England, gingerbread was a fairground treat with button and flower shapes found at Easter and animals and birds in autumn. Gingerbread was made with treacle syrup in England, while maple syrup was substituted in New England, and sorghum molasses provided the sweetening in the American South.

½ cup (48 g) ground ginger
¼ cup (24 g) ground cassia cinnamon
2 tablespoons (12 g) freshly ground black pepper

2 tablespoons (12 g) ground cardamom
1 tablespoon (6 g) ground allspice
1 teaspoon ground cloves

Combine all the ingredients in a small bowl and store in a tightly sealed container in a dark place for up to 3 months.

YIELD: About 1¼ cups (125 g)

▶ DID YOU KNOW?

In 1914, a German planter, Oscar Majus, brought cardamom plants to Guatemala when he realized that its climate and altitude were similar to the cardamom-growing Indian regions of Kerala and Tamil Nadu. Today, Guatemala is the world's biggest producer of cardamom. Until recently, the entire Guatemalan crop was exported to the Middle East, mostly to flavor coffee. Today, smugglers are bringing cardamom into Northern India through Pakistan, thereby creating an ongoing and heated spice war with Indian growers.

OTHER SUGGESTED USES

Use to season gingerbread cookies and gingerbread cake.

Sprinkle on baked apples or pears.

Add a pinch to eggnog and crème brûlée batter.

Add to pancake batter with golden raisins.

SWEDISH GINGERBREAD SPICE COOKIES

Making these cookies is a holiday tradition in Sweden. They belong to the large family of Northern European ginger and spice breads that date back to medieval times, when spices were so rare and expensive that they could only be used for the most important celebrations. Crushed-up cookies make a wonderful crumb crust for cheesecake or pumpkin or sweet potato pie. Use the crumbs to thicken the gravy for Beef Sauerbraten (page 91).

1¼ pounds (about 5 cups, or 568 g) unbleached all-purpose flour
1 tablespoon (14 g) baking soda
3 tablespoons (18 g) Gingerbread Spice Mix (page 88)
1 teaspoon fine sea salt
½ pound (2 sticks, or 227 g) unsalted butter, softened
¾ cup (150 g) granulated sugar
¾ cup (170 g) packed dark brown sugar

2 large eggs
1 egg yolk
¼ cup (80 g) honey
¼ cup (60 ml) heavy cream
1 lemon, zested
4 ounces (112 g) candied ginger, finely diced
1 egg white, lightly beaten with 1 tablespoon (15 ml) water, for egg wash
½ cup (100 g) raw or crystallized sugar, for sprinkling

1. Preheat the oven to 350°F (180°C, or gas mark 4). Line two 18 x 13-inch (45.7 x 33 cm) half sheet pans (or other large baking pans) with parchment paper or silicone baking mats.

2. In a bowl, whisk together the flour, baking soda, Gingerbread Spice Mix, and salt.

3. In the bowl of a standing mixer fitted with the paddle attachment, cream the butter, granulated sugar, and brown sugar until light and fluffy, 5 to 6 minutes. Beat in the eggs, yolk, honey, cream, and lemon zest.

4. Add the dry ingredients and candied ginger, beating only long enough for the dough to form a rough ball.

5. Scoop the dough into 48 balls about the size of a walnut. Arrange the dough balls in rows of three and two on the baking pans. Brush the cookies with the egg wash, then sprinkle with the raw sugar.

6. Bake the cookies for 7 to 8 minutes, or until lightly browned on the outside but still soft inside. Remove from the oven and, using the flat bottom of a cup or jar dipped in flour, flatten the cookies to about ⅛-inch (3 mm) thick. Place back in the oven and bake for 5 to 6 minutes longer, or until the cookies are crisp at the edges. (If baking two sheets at once, rotate the pans halfway through baking and bake a few minutes longer.) Cool the cookies to room temperature on a wire rack before serving.

YIELD: About 4 dozen 2-inch (5 cm) cookies

SPICEMASTER'S NOTE

The scooped cookie dough balls will freeze perfectly. Arrange them on a baking pan lined with parchment paper, wax paper, or a silicone mat and freeze. Once the cookies are completely frozen, transfer them to a resealable plastic freezer bag, squeeze out the excess air, and freeze.

PICKLING SPICE

This spice mix is used to make a pickling syrup for pickled prune plums and as a marinade for sauerbraten. (see page 20 for step-by-step photos); it may also be used to pickle firm peaches, sour cherries, and pears served as a relish for roasted or smoked poultry. Substitute all yellow mustard seeds if black (or brown) mustard seeds are not available.

- 4   cassia cinnamon sticks (3 inches, or 7.5 cm)
- 6   pieces whole dried gingerroot
- ¼ cup (45 g) black mustard seeds
- ¼ cup (45 g) yellow mustard seeds
- ¼ cup (24 g) coriander seeds
- ¼ cup (24 g) whole allspice berries
- ¼ cup (32 g) black peppercorns
- ¼ cup (40 g) dill seeds
- ¼ cup (40 g) fennel seeds
- 2   tablespoons (12 g) whole cloves
- 2   tablespoons (8 g) crushed mace blades
- ¼ cup (10 g) crumbled bay leaves
- 4   small whole dried chile peppers, such as chile arbol, crumbled

Place the cinnamon sticks in a heavy-duty resealable plastic bag or wrap in a clean towel. Using a hammer or mallet, break up the cinnamon sticks into small shards. Do the same for the dried gingerroot. Combine with the remaining ingredients. Store the Pickling Spice in a tightly sealed container away from the light for up to 8 months. When ready to use, for easy removal make a sachet by placing the pickling spices in cheesecloth and tying tightly with kitchen string with a long "tail" if desired.

YIELD: About 3 cups (270 g)

PICKLED SPICED PLUMS

- 3   cups (705 ml) cold water
- 2   cups (400 g) granulated sugar
- 4   cups (450 g) light brown sugar
- 4   cups (940 ml) apple cider vinegar
- ¼ cup (20 g) Pickling Spice
- 3   pounds (1.4 kg) prune plums, crabapples, or small, hard pears

1. Bring the water, both sugars, cider vinegar, and pickling spice to a boil in a nonreactive (not aluminum) pot.

2. Reduce the heat and simmer for 15 minutes to infuse the flavors.

3. Meanwhile, prick each plum in 2 or 3 places to keep them from bursting, then add to the liquid. Cook for 3 minutes or until the plums have softened. Remove from heat and cool to room temperature in the poaching liquid. Transfer to storage containers, preferably glass, ceramic, or stainless steel, and refrigerate for 1 week to cure before serving. The plums will keep for about 2 months refrigerated. If desired, transfer to sterilized canning jars and process according to the manufacturer's directions for longer storage.

YIELD: 3 cups (1.4 kg)

OTHER SUGGESTED USES

Use to pickle meats such as corned beef.

Use to pickle vegetables such as cabbage, okra, onions, and mushrooms.

Use to pickle oily fish such as salmon and herring.

Use to season the liquid for poaching shrimp, crabs, and crayfish.

BEEF SAUERBRATEN WITH GINGERSNAPS

Sauerbraten gets its name from the German *sauer*, or sour, and *braten*, for roast meat. It is a German pot roast that can be prepared with a variety of meats—usually beef, but also game meats, mutton, pork, and traditionally, horsemeat. A large tougher cut of meat is marinated anywhere from three to as much as ten days in a mixture of an acid such as vinegar or wine, Pickling Spice, and other seasonings. Sauerbraten is one of Germany's national dishes and is often accompanied by braised red cabbage and potato dumplings or spaetzle noodles to soak up the savory juices. The crumbled gingersnaps (see page 89) used to soak up the juices are one traditional variation.

1   cup (235 ml) cider vinegar
1   large onion, coarsely chopped
1   lemon, cut into wedges
¼   cup (28 g) Pickling Spice (page 90)
1   tablespoon (18 g) sea salt
1   quart (940 ml) cold water
1   beef bottom round roast, trimmed and tied (4 to 5 pounds or 1.8 to 2.3 kg)

2   cups (470 ml) beef, chicken, or vegetable stock, homemade or store-bought
¼   cup (60 ml) vegetable oil
¼   cup (30 g) all-purpose flour
2   ounces (½ cup, or 56 g) crushed Swedish Gingerbread Spice Cookies (page 89) or store-bought gingersnaps
¼   cup (60 g) packed dark brown sugar

1. Starting 3 days ahead of time, combine the vinegar, onion, lemon wedges, Pickling Spice, salt, and cold water in a medium pot. Bring to a boil, then cool to room temperature.

2. Place the beef in a large bowl and add the cooled marinade, which should just cover the meat. Top the meat with a plate to keep it submerged in the marinade. Cover and marinate, refrigerated, for 3 days, turning the beef once a day.

3. When ready to cook, preheat the oven to 350°F (180°C, or gas mark 4).

4. Remove the beef from the marinade, reserving the marinade (not strained) in the refrigerator. Pat the beef dry and place in a roasting pan just large enough to hold the meat, fat-side (the outer side) up. Roast for 1 hour and then reduce the oven temperature to 275°F (140°C, or gas mark 1). Continue roasting until tender to the center when pierced, about 5 hours. Remove the beef from the oven and transfer to a cutting board.

5. Deglaze the browned bits from the roasting pan by pouring in the beef stock and place back in the oven for about 15 minutes. Scrape the softened browned bits from the pan using a wooden spoon, pour into a bowl or large measuring cup, and reserve.

6. In a large heavy skillet, combine the oil and flour. Cook over medium heat, stirring constantly, until deep brown, about 10 minutes. Gradually whisk in the reserved marinade and pan juices. Bring to a boil and cook over medium heat, stirring often, until the sauce has thickened, about 10 minutes, skimming off foam as necessary. Add the cookie crumbs and brown sugar and stir well to combine. Strain the sauce through a wire sieve or a French wire chinois, pressing firmly on the solids to extract all the juices. Discard the solids.

7. Ladle about 2 cups (470 ml) of the strained sauce into a large baking dish. Slice the beef thinly against the grain and arrange in layers in the baking dish, spooning sauce in between each layer. Pour the remaining sauce over the top.

8. When ready to serve, preheat the oven to 350°F (180°C, or gas mark 4). Cover and bake until the beef is heated through, about 30 minutes.

YIELD: 8 to 10 servings

TEMPERO DA ESSÊNCIA

This is a traditional Portuguese recipe for an herb and spice blend hot with African piri piri chiles that is typically used for seasoning meats. Piri piri chiles, also known as African bird's eye pepper or malagueta pepper, is a small cultivar of *Capsicum frutescens* and grows both wild and domesticated. It was carried across the Atlantic by the Portuguese, who also brought it to Angola in Africa and to Goa in India when both were Portuguese colonies. Piri piri means "pepper pepper" in Swahili.

2 tablespoons (16 g) ground piri piri chiles (substitute ground, dried red chiles such as cayenne, chile ancho powder, or hot paprika)
2 tablespoons (36 g) sea salt
¼ cup (36 g) garlic powder

2 tablespoons (12 g) freshly ground black pepper
2 tablespoons (12 g) ground cumin
2 tablespoons (14 g) onion powder
2 tablespoons (4 g) dried oregano
2 tablespoons (12 g) dried thyme

Combine all the ingredients in a small bowl and mix well. Store in a tightly sealed container away from the light for up to 4 months.

YIELD: About 1 cup (175 g)

PORTUGUESE GAMBAS MOZAMBIQUE

A legacy of Portugal's past as a nation of exploring seafarers, this dish comes from Mozambique, where small, fiery hot piri piri peppers are a signature culinary accent. Look for wild shrimp, which have far more flavor and firmer texture than often-bland farmed shrimp. Although prepeeled and frozen shrimp (IQF shrimp) are easier to use, much flavor is lost in the process. Here we use whole, head-on shrimp for juicy succulence. Serve the saucy shrimp in bowls with crusty Portuguese bread to soak up the delicious juices. Substitute beer for the wine if desired.

¼ cup (56 g) unsalted butter
1 small onion, finely diced
4 large cloves garlic, minced
1 cup (235 ml) dry white wine
1 lemon, juiced
1 teaspoon sea salt
2 tablespoons (22 g) Tempero da Essência

2 pounds (908 g) large firm shrimp (21-25 count), peeled and deveined with last tail shell section left on
1 tablespoon (15 ml) bottled piri piri hot sauce (substitute Tabasco or any chile-vinegar hot sauce)
Small handful cilantro, chopped
Small handful Italian parsley, chopped

1. Melt the butter in a skillet. Add onion and garlic and cook over medium heat until the onion has softened, about 4 minutes. Add the white wine, lemon juice, salt, and Tempero da Essência and cook until thickened and syrupy, about 4 minutes.
2. Toss in the shrimp and hot sauce and toss to coat with the pan juices. Cook over medium heat until the shrimp just turn opaque and start to curl. Add the cilantro and parsley and toss to combine. Spoon the shrimp and cooking juices into bowls and serve immediately.

YIELD: 4 servings

OTHER SUGGESTED USES

Rub chicken, beef skirt steak or hanger steak, shrimp, or whole fish with this spicy seasoning mix before grilling or roasting.

Add to cooked lentils, chickpeas, or beans.

Toss with buttered or olive-oiled fresh popcorn.

SPEZIE FORTI

This recipe comes from renowned Tuscan chef Cesare Casella. He says, "*Spezie forte* translates to 'robust spice' and was traditionally used by Tuscan butchers to prepare sausages. Each butcher has his proprietary blend of these aromatic spices, and I use mine in many of my dishes at Salumeria Rosi Parmacotto. I use spezie forte in my slow-cooked spareribs and house-made sausages, dusted on chicken wings, and even in soups. Another fun fact—many Italians consider it to be a powerful aphrodisiac, and I like to refer to it as 'Tuscan Viagra.'" Chef Casella weighs his spices using metric quantities for greater accuracy, especially when making larger batches. Here we measure using tablespoons, but if you have a good scale, weigh out at 15 grams per spice.

- 2 tablespoons (15 g) ground allspice
- 2 tablespoons (15 g) grated nutmeg
- 2 tablespoons (15 g) ground cinnamon
- 2 tablespoons (15 g) ground mace
- 2 tablespoons (15 g) ground juniper berries
- 2 tablespoons (15 g) ground coriander
- 2 tablespoons (15 g) ground cloves
- 2 tablespoons (15 g) ground star anise or ground aniseed
- 2 tablespoons (15 g) paprika
- 2 tablespoons (15 g) freshly ground black pepper

Combine all the ingredients and store in a tightly sealed container in a dark place for up to 4 months.

YIELD: About 1¼ cups (120 g)

▶ VARIATION

I recommend increasing the amount of ground juniper to ¼ cup (30 g) and using 2 teaspoons (6 g) of cloves instead of 2 tablespoons (15 g) for an earthier, woodsy flavor.

OTHER SUGGESTED USES

Use to season pork and veal spareribs before slow-roasting or grilling.

Add to chicken liver pâté.

Add to the pan when cooking fresh Italian sausages.

Add to braised beef dishes like stracotto.

94 THE MAGIC OF SPICE BLENDS

TUSCAN CHICKEN LIVER SPREAD ON ROSEMARY CROSTINI

In Tuscany, every *osteria* (country-style restaurant) serves its own version of this pâté as part of its antipasto offerings, accompanied always by a glass of local red wine. Here chicken livers are enriched with Italian cured, not smoked, bacon called pancetta, and flavored with Spezie Forte and umami-rich dried porcini mushrooms and chopped to a fine, though not puréed, consistency. The spread is best served warm on crostini toasts but is also delicious served chilled or at room temperature spread on flatbread crisps. Look for chicken livers from grain-fed chickens, which will be lighter in color and milder in flavor than those from commercial-grade chickens.

FOR PÂTÉ

- 1 ounce (about ¼ cup, or 28 g) dried porcini mushrooms
- 1 pound (454 g) chicken livers
- 2 shallots, chopped
- 1 rib celery, chopped
- 1 small carrot, chopped
  Handful Italian parsley with small stems, chopped
- 1 tablespoon (7 g) Spezie Forte (page 94)
- 4 ounces (112 g) pancetta, chopped
- 2 tablespoons (28 g) unsalted butter
- 2 tablespoons (30 ml) extra-virgin olive oil
- 2 teaspoons (12 g) sea salt
- ¼ cup (60 ml) dry white wine
- ½ cup (55 g) soft breadcrumbs
- ½ lemon, juiced (1 to 1½ tablespoons, or 15 to 23 ml)

FOR CROSTINI

- 1 loaf crusty Italian bread or French baguette, preferably stale
- ¼ cup (60 ml) extra-virgin olive oil
- 1 tablespoon (2 g) finely chopped rosemary
- 2 cloves garlic, minced

TO MAKE THE PÂTÉ

1. Soak the dried porcini in just enough warm water to cover until softened, about 30 minutes. Scoop the mushrooms from the water and chop finely. Strain the mushroom soaking liquid through a dampened paper towel placed in a wire sieve to remove any sand and mix back with the chopped mushrooms.

2. Rinse the chicken livers under cold water, drain well, and pat dry.

3. In a large skillet, sauté the shallots, celery, carrot, parsley, Spezie Forte, and pancetta in the butter and olive oil until softened but not browned, about 5 minutes. Season with salt. When the vegetables are soft, add the chicken livers, chopped porcini and strained soaking liquid, and white wine. Cook over high heat until the livers are pink inside, but not fully cooked, about 5 minutes. Turn off the heat and allow the mixture to cool.

4. Ideally, set up a meat grinder with a large-holed grinding plate and grind to a rough consistency. Alternatively, transfer to a large cutting board and chop to small bits with some texture. Or pulse in a food processor to a rough consistency without turning the mixture into mush.

5. Transfer the mixture to a bowl, add the breadcrumbs and lemon juice, and stir to combine. The mixture should be soft and juicy, with just enough body to hold its shape.

TO MAKE THE CROSTINI

1. Preheat the oven to 350°F (180°C, or gas mark 4). Cut the bread on the diagonal into slices about ⅜-inch (1 cm) thick. Arrange in a single layer on a baking tray. Combine the oil, rosemary, and garlic in a small bowl and brush the mixture on the bread slices. Turn the slices over and repeat, brushing lightly.

2. Toast until golden brown, about 12 minutes. Serve with the warm pâté spooned on top.

YIELD: About 1½ pounds or 3½ cups (680 g), 12 to 16 servings

SPICEMASTER'S NOTE

Two tablespoons (10 g) whole juniper will yield about 2 tablespoons (15 g) ground. Grind in a spice grinder to a coarse texture or crush in a mortar and pestle. Once ground, juniper berries quickly lose their fragrance, so only grind what you need

To clean a spice grinder, crumble a slice of stale bread (the end piece works well) and run it through the grinder. The bread will absorb the spice oils in the grinder. Once ground, discard the bread.

BLENDS FROM THE
INDIAN
SUBCONTINENT

Fragrant and aromatic, Indian cuisine relies on an enormous variety and quantity of spices. Native Indian spice, include black and green cardamom, black cumin, black and long pepper, true cinnamon, curry leaf, Indian bay leaf, and turmeric. Ginger Is thought to have originated in southern China but half the world's production is now in India. Chiles, brought from the New World by the Portuguese, are used generously in South India and Sri Lanka. Half of the world's chiles are produced in India but 90 percent are consumed locally.

A strong Arab influence is seen in the use of aromatic spices like ajwain, cumin, coriander, and saffron in Northern India and Pakistan. Indian spice blends are creations that enhance specific dishes, many based on fresh ginger, garlic, and green chiles. Dry blends include Bengali Panch Phoron, Northern Indian Garam Masala, Balti Masala, and Southern Indian Sambar Podi.

BASIC CURRY POWDER

There are countless variations of curry powder, which is a spice mix of widely varying composition based on South Asian cuisine. Curry powder and the contemporary English use of the word *curry* as a dish of various ingredients seasoned with curry powder are Western inventions created to satisfy the tastes of British colonials returning to Great Britain from India. Curry powder is related closest to South Indian and Sri Lankan Sambar Podi (page 108). Curry gets its name from the Tamil word *kari*, meaning "sauce" or "relish." Curry-like dishes featuring ginger, garlic, and turmeric were known in the Indus Valley civilization more than 4,000 years ago, which scientists have discovered by using powerful laboratory microscopes to identify the ingredients of ancient meals. This curry powder is fragrant and easy to make. Toasting the spices first brings out their deep, complex flavor.

½ cup (40 g) coriander seeds, preferably Indian
¼ cup (40 g) cumin seeds
1 tablespoon (8 g) black peppercorns
1 section (1 inch, or 2.5 cm) true cinnamon quill, crushed
1 teaspoon whole cloves
2 teaspoons (6 g) decorticated cardamom

¼ cup (40 g) ground turmeric
2 tablespoons (12 g) ground ginger
2 tablespoons (18 g) ground mustard
2 tablespoons (25 g) ground fenugreek
2 teaspoons (6 g) ground cayenne

1. Heat a dry skillet over medium heat. Add the coriander, cumin, peppercorns, cinnamon, cloves, and cardamom. Toast until fragrant, while constantly stirring, about 3 minutes. Cool to room temperature and then grind in a spice grinder, blender, or mortar and pestle.

2. Mix well with the remaining ingredients. Store in a tightly sealed container in a dark, cool place for up to 3 months.

YIELD: About 1¾ cups (175 g)

INDONESIAN CURRY KETCHUP

It's all the rage in Germany and Holland—served on wurst and other sausages. It's time to discover this Indonesian condiment that is so much more interesting than ordinary tomato ketchup. Look for it in former Dutch colonies such as Aruba, where every supermarket carries several brands. The black cardamom pods add a mysterious smoky flavor to the condiment, while star anise adds spicy sweet fragrance and cloves a warm undertone.

6 black cardamom pods
12 star anise pods
1 teaspoon whole cloves
¼ cup (60 ml) vegetable oil
1 small onion, diced
4 cloves garlic, minced
1 piece (4 inches, or 10 cm)
 fresh gingerroot, peeled and
 chopped (2 ounces, or 56 g)

2 cans (28 ounces, or 784 g)
 crushed tomatoes
2 cups (470 ml) water
2 cups (470 ml) apple cider vinegar
1 cup (225 g) packed dark brown sugar
½ cup (50 g) Basic Curry Powder
1 teaspoon hot red pepper flakes
1 tablespoon (18 g) sea salt

1. Wrap the black cardamom, star anise, and whole cloves in a piece of cheesecloth, tie shut, and reserve.

2. Warm the oil in a large saucepan over medium heat. Sauté the onion, garlic, and ginger until softened but not browned, about 5 minutes. Add the tomatoes, water, vinegar, brown sugar, curry powder, red pepper flakes, sea salt, and the cheesecloth spice packet to the pan. Stir to combine. Bring to a boil, reduce the heat to low, and simmer for about 45 minutes, stirring often, until the mixture thickens enough to hold its shape.

3. Fish out the spice packet and discard. Blend the sauce in a blender or food processor until smooth. Cool to room temperature and then transfer to storage containers or jars and refrigerate for up to 3 months.

YIELD: About 3 quarts (24 kg)

BALTI MASALA SPICE MIX

Balti cooking became popular during the 1970s in England, especially in Birmingham, where every restaurant developed its own mix of spices and style of serving the curry. Balti curry is typically served in a thin, spun steel, wok-like "Balti bowl" and is on the dry side because most of the liquid evaporates while cooking. This type of curry may have originated in the northern Pakistan region of Baltistan in Kashmir, and then immigrants brought it to Britain. Other common flavorings for Balti masala include dried rose petals, dried spearmint leaves, bay leaves, and saffron. The process of creating a Balti Masala Spice Mix is shown step-by-step on page 22.

2 **cassia cinnamon quills (4 inches, or 10 cm)**
½ **cup (40 g) coriander seeds, preferably Indian**
4 **black cardamom pods, crushed**
8 **whole cloves**
6 **tablespoons (60 g) cumin seeds**
2 **tablespoons (15 g) aniseed**
2 **tablespoons (22 g) black mustard seeds**

1 **tablespoon (12 g) fenugreek seeds**
2 **teaspoons (5 g) ajwain seeds**
2 **teaspoons (6 g) decorticated cardamom seeds**
2 **tablespoons (5 g) crushed dried fenugreek leaves (methi)**
2 **tablespoons (2 g) crushed dried curry leaves**
1 **tablespoon (5 g) nigella seeds**

1. Using a hammer or mallet, crush the cinnamon sticks into small shards. Heat a large dry skillet over medium heat. Add the cassia, coriander seeds, black cardamom pods, and cloves. Roast the spices until fragrant and lightly toasted, shaking the pan constantly. Remove from the heat, cool to room temperature, and then crush in a mortar and pestle or grind to a slightly coarse powder.
2. Heat the same skillet again. Add the cumin seeds, aniseed, black mustard seeds, fenugreek, ajwain, and cardamom seeds and roast until fragrant and lightly toasted, shaking the pan constantly. Remove from the heat, cool to room temperature, and then crush in a mortar and pestle or grind to a slightly coarse powder. If desired, strain the spices through a wire sieve for a finer texture.
3. Crush or grind the fenugreek leaves and curry leaves and combine well with the spices. Stir in the nigella seeds.
4. Store in a tightly sealed container away from the light for up to 6 months.

YIELD: About 1½ cups (165 g)

BEEF BALTI CURRY

Inexpensive but flavorful beef chuck from the shoulder makes the best-tasting rich curry, here infused with the complex flavors of Balti Masala Spice Mix. You may substitute tender beef stir-fry strips, but cook them only until cooked through, about 15 minutes, or the beef will be dry. Substitute lamb shoulder cubes or cubed boneless, skinless chicken thigh for the beef, if desired. A scattering of brilliant red pomegranate seeds adds sparkle and bright crunch to the dish, accented with fresh green cilantro sprigs. Serve with steamed basmati rice, yogurt raita, and Indian chutneys or pickles. The beef and sauce freeze perfectly.

OTHER SUGGESTED USES

Add to curried chicken, beef, lamb, or vegetable dishes.

Add to rice and rice dishes such as biryani.

Rub on squash or sweet potato wedges or cubes with a little oil and then roast.

FOR MARINADE

2 tablespoons (14 g) Balti Masala Spice Mix (page 100)
2 tablespoons (30 ml) vegetable oil
1 lemon, juiced
1 tablespoon (10 g) ground turmeric
1 tablespoon (5 g) nigella seeds
2 teaspoons (4 g) ground cinnamon
2 teaspoons (12 g) sea salt

FOR BEEF

3 pounds (1.4 kg) boneless beef chuck cubes
2 medium onions, halved and thinly sliced
1 section (3 inches, or 7.5 cm) fresh gingerroot, peeled and thinly sliced
6 large cloves garlic
2 tablespoons (14 g) Balti Masala Spice Mix (page 100)
2 tablespoons (30 g) dark brown sugar
2 cups (360 g) chopped tomatoes, fresh or canned
   Pomegranate seeds and cilantro sprigs (optional), for garnish

TO MAKE THE MARINADE:
Starting 1 day ahead, combine the marinade ingredients and mix well.

TO MAKE THE BEEF:
1. Combine the beef cubes with the marinade, transfer to a large bowl, cover, and refrigerate overnight.
2. The next day, remove the beef from the refrigerator and allow it to come to room temperature, about 1 hour.
3. Preheat the oven to 425°F (220°C, or gas mark 7).
4. Transfer the beef cubes to a roasting pan just large enough to hold them. Roast the beef until brown, about 30 minutes. Transfer the beef to a large braising pan. Add the onions to the pan and cook over medium heat until softened, about 30 minutes, stirring often.
5. Meanwhile, combine the ginger, garlic, the Balti Masala, and brown sugar in the bowl of a food processor or blender. Blend until fairly smooth. Add to the beef along with the tomatoes and simmer for 30 minutes longer, or until the beef is quite tender and the sauce has reduced.
6. Scatter the beef with the pomegranate seeds and cilantro and serve immediately.

YIELD: 6 to 8 servings

KHOTACHIWADI EAST INDIAN BOTTLE MASALA

This unique recipe comes from the East Indian community who were the original settlers of Mumbai and traditionally Christian, living in the tiny serene heritage village of Khotachiwadi, hidden in the center of the city's crowds and noise. There, charming houses are built in the old Portuguese style with courtyards and an external staircase to access the upstairs bedrooms. The women of the local families practice the art of pounding spices into a blend known as bottle masala that is unique to each family and passed down from mother to daughter. The complex mix is made in large enough quantities to last the whole year. The spices are roasted in clay pots over a wood fire, hand-pounded using wooden mallets, and finally packed in glass bottles. Stone flower, a dried edible lichen, may be found online and at Indian markets but may be omitted. The original recipe called for 1 tablespoon (2 g) maipatri, or mugwort (*Artemisia vulgaris*), which may be difficult to find and may be omitted.

SPICEMASTER'S NOTE

This recipe is based on glowing red Kashmiri chiles, which are medium-hot and valued for their vibrant red color. When roasted, they impart an exotic aroma to vegetable dishes and rice pilaf and biryani. Substitute a mixture of milder New Mexico or California red chiles and small hot chiles such as chile arbol for the Kashmiri chiles. Look for whole and easier-to-use powdered Kashmiri chile in Indian markets and from online vendors.

- 3 tablespoons (15 g) coriander seeds, preferably Indian
- 1 section (1 inch, or 2.5 cm) true cinnamon quill, crushed
- 4 teaspoons (13 g) cumin seeds
- 2 tablespoons (18 g) sesame seeds
- 2 tablespoons (15 g) poppy seeds
- 2 tablespoons (22 g) yellow mustard seeds
- 1 tablespoon (2 g) stone flower (optional)
- 2 teaspoons (6 g) black peppercorns
- 4 star anise pods
- 2 teaspoons (6 g) fennel seeds
- 2 teaspoons (8 g) fenugreek seeds
- 2 teaspoons (3 g) black cumin or more cumin seeds
- 1 teaspoon whole cloves
- ¼ whole nutmeg (crush with a mallet or hammer)
- 2 blades mace
- 2 teaspoons (1.5 g) crumbled Indian bay leaves or bay laurel leaves
- 2 ounces (56 g) Kashmiri chile powder
- ¼ cup (30 g) whole wheat flour
- 2 tablespoons (20 g) ground turmeric

1. Heat a dry skillet over medium heat. Roast the spices (everything except the Kashmiri chile powder, whole wheat flour, and turmeric) until lightly browned and fragrant, about 3 minutes. Remove from the skillet and cool to room temperature.

2. Add the Kashmiri chile powder, whole wheat flour, and turmeric to the skillet and roast briefly, about 1 minute, until lightly browned and fragrant. Remove from the skillet and cool to room temperature.

3. Grind the roasted whole spices to a slightly coarse powder in a mortar and pestle, a spice or coffee grinder, or a blender. Combine well with the chile powder, flour, and turmeric.

4. Pack into glass jars or metal tins using a funnel. Store in a dark, cool place for up to 1 year.

YIELD: 2½ cups (300 g)

▶ DID YOU KNOW?

Stone flower is a feathery lichen, known as *dagad phool* or *kalpasi*, with a strong, sweet aroma that is released when the lichen hits the hot oil of a cooking pan. It is used in small quantities to impart unique flavor to masalas in the Southern Indian region of Chettinad.

LONVAS CHICKEN DRUMSTICKS AND PUMPKIN CURRY

This curry is typical of the East Indian community and is traditionally made with bottle masala and the speckled green-skinned ash gourd, or *petha* in Hindi, which can keep in the pantry for as long as one year. It is also known as winter gourd, winter melon, or white pumpkin. Here we use dense, meaty pumpkin such as Japanese kuri or Spanish calabaza. The curry may be prepared with beef or mutton instead of the drumsticks and cauliflower or okra instead of the ash gourd. This old Mumbai Christian community also makes pork lonvas and prawn lonvas. Serve the curry over steamed basmati rice.

3 pounds (1.4 kg) chicken drumsticks
1 teaspoon sea salt
6 tablespoons (90 ml) ghee (clarified butter) or vegetable oil, divided
½ cup (120 ml) water
3 large cloves garlic, crushed
1 pound (454 g) Japanese kuri squash, calabaza, or ash gourd, peeled and cubed

3 tablespoons (22 g) Khotachiwadi East Indian Bottle Masala (page 102)
1 can (13.5 ounces, or 378 g) rich unsweetened coconut milk
2 tablespoons (36 g) tamarind purée (see page 83)

1. Season the chicken with the salt. Heat 3 tablespoons (45 ml) of the ghee in a large Dutch oven and then brown the chicken well, working in batches if necessary. Add the water, cover, and cook the drumsticks until tender, about 20 minutes. Remove the chicken from the pan and reserve.

2. Wipe out the pan, add the remaining 3 tablespoons (45 ml) ghee and the garlic and heat together until the garlic is fragrant. Add the squash and bottle masala and sauté until the squash has softened, about 10 minutes. Add the reserved chicken and the coconut milk and bring to a slow boil. Cook together until the sauce has thickened slightly, about 5 minutes, then stir in the tamarind purée. Allow the curry to rest for a few minutes before serving.

YIELD: 6 to 8 servings

OTHER SUGGESTED USES

Use to season chicken, shrimp, pork, or vegetable curries.

Add to cooked lentils or chickpeas.

Use to season rice or potatoes.

Add to tomato sauce, soups, lentil dishes, and to top pizza.

GARAM MASALA

Garam masala is the best known of India's spice mixes and originates in Northern India's Persian-derived Mogul cuisine. This versatile mix of roasted spices is made in a variety of styles across the Indian subcontinent. It is conceptually related to Turkish baharat, Chinese Five-Spice Powder, and even French quatre épices, which are all based on black peppercorns combined with sweet aromatic spices. In Pakistan, onions are fried until golden brown and then the garam masala is added to the hot oil to bring out its flavor before being added to rice pilau (pilaf). The Indian coriander seeds used here are lemon-shaped, rather than round, as in the more common Mediterranean coriander. Its flavor is brighter and more lemony than the European variety.

- 3 true cinnamon sticks (2 to 3 inches, or 5 to 7.5 cm)
- ½ cup (50 g) white or green cardamom pods, 3 tablespoons (30 g) decorticated cardamom, or 2 tablespoons (12 g) ground cardamom
- 6 bay leaves
- ¾ cup (60 g) coriander seeds, preferably Indian
- ½ cup (80 g) cumin seeds
- ¼ cup (32 g) black peppercorns
- 1 tablespoon (5 g) whole cloves

1. Break up the cinnamon sticks into small shards by placing in a heavy-duty resealable plastic bag or a clean towel and using a hammer or meat mallet to crush. If using whole cardamom, break open the pods, remove the hard black seeds, and discard the pods. Crumble the bay leaves.

2. Heat a small, dry skillet, preferably uncoated (such as steel or cast iron), over high heat. Add the cinnamon, cardamom seeds, bay leaves, coriander seeds, cumin seeds, peppercorns, and cloves. Toast, shaking the pan occasionally, until the spices are lightly browned and fragrant. Watch the spices carefully at this point so they don't turn black and become bitter.

3. Remove from the heat and cool the spices to room temperature. Grind to a powder in a small coffee grinder, preferably one reserved for spices. Alternatively, crush the seeds using a mortar and pestle. Store in a tightly sealed container away from the light for up to 4 months.

YIELD: About 2 cups (220 g)

OTHER SUGGESTED USES

Use to season a multitude of Pakistani and Northern and Southern Indian dishes, including kebabs, biryani rice dishes, breads, and chutneys.

▶ OTHER SPICES USED IN GARAM MASALA

- Ajwain (carom) seeds
- Anardana (dried pomegranate seeds)
- Black cumin (kala jeera)
- Cubeb pepper
- Fennel seeds
- Mace
- Mustard seeds
- Nutmeg
- Stone flower (lichen)
- Turmeric
- White peppercorns

TOMATO KASUNDI CHUTNEY

This hot and spicy mustard-based tomato chutney comes from Bengal, where it is known as *tamtar kasundi*. Its various savory and spicy flavors maintain their distinct characters, yet, at the same time, seamlessly blend with one another. In India, the kasundi would accompany a main dish with naan or paratha bread. It's the perfect dip for fried foods such as fish, samosas, and pakoras. Try it on burgers, grilled fish or chicken, or as a spread for turkey and tuna sandwiches.

1   medium onion, coarsely chopped
4   large cloves garlic, coarsely chopped
4   hot green chiles, such as jalapeño or serrano, seeded and sliced
1   section fresh gingerroot,(2 inches, or 5 cm) peeled and sliced
¼   cup (60 ml) mustard oil (available in Indian markets), or ¼ cup (60 ml) vegetable oil plus 2 tablespoons (18 g) ground mustard
¼   cup (44 g) black mustard seeds
2   tablespoons (14 g) Garam Masala (page 104)
2   tablespoons (20 g) turmeric
1   tablespoon (6 g) ground cumin
1   teaspoon ground cardamom
1   teaspoon ground cinnamon, preferably true cinnamon
1   cup (300 g) tamarind purée (see page 83)
2   cans (28 ounces, or 784 g each) chopped plum tomatoes or 4 pounds (1.8 kg) ripe plum tomatoes, skinned, seeded, and chopped
2   tablespoons (30 g) dark brown sugar
2   teaspoons (12 g) sea salt
1   bunch cilantro, chopped

1. Combine the onion, garlic, chiles, and ginger in the bowl of a food processor and grind to a slightly chunky paste.

2. In a large heavy-bottomed pot, heat the oil, add the mustard seeds, and cover, cooking until the seeds pop. Add the Garam Masala, turmeric, cumin, cardamom, and cinnamon to the pan, stir to combine, and then add the onion-garlic-chile paste. Fry the paste in the spices until fragrant, about 3 minutes, stirring constantly.

3. Add the tamarind purée, tomatoes, brown sugar, and salt and cook over low heat until thickened, stirring frequently, about 30 minutes, adding water if the sauce is overly thick. The oil will rise to the top when the kasundi has thickened sufficiently. Remove from the heat and stir in the cilantro. Cool to room temperature and then transfer to a storage container. Refrigerate for up to 4 months.

YIELD: About 1 quart (900 g)

PANCH PHORON

Panch means "five," and this five-seed mixture from Bengal, a region famous all over India for its distinct cuisine, is also known as Bengali five spice. The spices are usually fried in oil or ghee (clarified butter) until they start popping, a technique known as *tempering*. After tempering, other ingredients are added to the fried spices to be coated in the mixture. Panch Phoron, which is not hot, owes its flavor to the contrast between sweet fennel and bitter fenugreek seeds along with earthy cumin, acrid nigella, and umami-rich radhuni, a local spice with celery flavor in the celery family and closely related to ajwain. Mustard seeds are the most common substitute.

¼ cup (44 g) black mustard seeds
¼ cup (20 g) nigella seeds
¼ cup (40 g) cumin seeds

2 tablespoons (25 g) crushed fenugreek seeds
¼ cup (40 g) fennel seeds

Combine all the ingredients and store in a tightly sealed container away from light and heat for up to 6 months.

YIELD: About 1¼ cups (175 g)

GOLD POTATOES WITH PANCH PHORON

The asafetida called for here imparts a potent, trufflelike aroma to the potatoes while the Panch Phoron spices, which cling to the potatoes as they fry, add resinous, sweet, earthy, and savory notes to the dish. Turmeric enhances the natural gold color of the potatoes. The most flavorful potatoes to use are gold varieties such as Yukon or Finnish, but choose larger potatoes with thick skins, which will be starchier. Substitute russet potatoes for a firmer texture.

2 pounds (454 g) gold potatoes, peeled if skin is thick
1 cup (120 ml) vegetable oil
1 teaspoon asafetida

6 tablespoons (27 g) Panch Phoron
2 tablespoons (10 g) turmeric
2 teaspoons sea salt

1. Cut the potatoes into ½-inches to ¾-inch (1.3 to 2 cm) dice.
2. Heat the oil in a wok or a heavy skillet over medium heat. Add the asafetida, stir to flavor the oil, and then quickly add the Panch Phoron and the potatoes. Cook together over medium heat until the potatoes are almost cooked through and lightly colored. Add the turmeric and continue to fry until the potatoes are golden and the spices cling to the potatoes.
3. Scoop the potatoes from the oil using a slotted spoon or wire skimmer and drain well on a wire rack placed over a baking pan or on paper towels. Transfer to a bowl and toss with the salt. Serve immediately while still piping hot.

YIELD: 4 to 6 servings

OTHER SUGGESTED USES

Use as a coating on roast meats.

Sprinkle on Indian breads.

Sprinkle on hearty vegetables, especially eggplant, green beans, potatoes, okra, and cauliflower.

SPICEMASTER'S NOTE

Asafetida is the notoriously smelly, dried yellow-brownish resin extracted from the root of a plant (*Ferula assafoetida*) that grows wild from the Eastern Mediterranean to Central Asia. Asafetida gets its name from two languages: *assa* from Farsi, meaning "resin," and Latin *foetidus*, meaning "stinky." To those who have become accustomed to it, asafetida is intriguingly stimulating, with an earthy, trufflelike aroma. The pure resin is the strongest form, but the powder, known as *hing* in Indian markets, is easier to use. The yellow powder is milder than the gray. Asafetida resin lasts indefinitely, but in powdered form it loses much of its aroma after about 6 months.

ALLEPPEY

SAMBAR PODI

Starting with whole spices and lightly toasting them before grinding yields a more fragrant, fresher mixture. If you can find the lemon-shaped Indian coriander seeds instead of the more common round Mediterranean coriander seeds, use them. Dark gold in color, Alleppey turmeric, from Alleppey, India, is preferable to common turmeric. Sambar Podi (sambar powder) is indispensable to Southern Indian cooking. Its most important element is coriander, with cumin next on the list, as well as black mustard seeds, fenugreek seeds, hot chiles, and roasted legumes such as lentils or split chickpeas, which add flavor and thickening power to the mix.

- 6 tablespoons (30 g) coriander seeds, preferably Indian
- 3 tablespoons (30 g) cumin seeds
- 3 tablespoons (30 g) chana dal (small split chickpeas—found in Indian markets)
- 1 tablespoon (11 g) black mustard seeds
- 1 tablespoon (12 g) fenugreek seeds
- 2 teaspoons (6 g) black peppercorns
- 1 teaspoon whole cloves
- 1 teaspoon decorticated cardamom
- 1 section (2 inches, or 5 cm) true cinnamon, crumbled
- 1 whole dried red chile pepper, such as chile arbol, crumbled with seeds discarded
- ¼ cup (40 g) ground turmeric
- 2 tablespoons (12 g) ground dried ginger
- 2 teaspoons (6 g) ground yellow asafetida

1. Heat a small, dry skillet, preferably uncoated (such as steel or cast iron), over high heat. Add the coriander, cumin, chana dal, mustard, fenugreek, peppercorns, cloves, cardamom, cinnamon, and dried chile. Toast, shaking the pan occasionally, until the spices are lightly browned and fragrant. Watch the spices carefully at this point so they don't turn black and become bitter.

2. Cool to room temperature and then grind in a spice grinder or mortar and pestle.

3. Combine with the turmeric, dried ginger, and asafetida. If desired, strain through a wire sieve for a finer texture.

4. Store in a tightly sealed container away from the light for up to 4 months.

YIELD: About 2 cups (220 g)

SRI LANKAN COCONUT VEGETABLE CURRY WITH CASHEWS AND YAMS

Sri Lanka has long been renowned for its fragrant spices, especially top-quality true cinnamon, which is produced there and exported mainly to the United States, Mexico, Peru, and Colombia. Since ancient times, traders from all over the world who came to Sri Lanka brought their native cuisines to the island, resulting in a rich diversity of cooking styles and techniques. Coconut is an important ingredient, as are fiery hot chiles, which the locals develop a tolerance for. In this mixed vegetable curry, cashews—brought to the region by the Portuguese from Brazil, where it is native—and toasted unsweetened coconut add richness and nutty flavor, while rich coconut milk yields a creamy sauce.

1 pound (454 g) yams, peeled, quartered lengthwise, and cut into ½-inch (1.3 cm) thick slices
1 medium eggplant, peeled if desired and cut into 1-inch (2.5 cm) dice
½ pound (227 g) young okra (substitute green beans), stems removed, cut in half lengthwise
1 small cauliflower, cored and cut into small florets
1 medium sweet onion, diced
2 teaspoons (12 g) sea salt
2 tablespoons (16 g) grated fresh gingerroot
3 cloves garlic, minced
3 tablespoons (45 ml) lime juice
½ cup (40 g) shredded dried unsweetened coconut
¼ pound (1 cup, or 114 g) toasted cashews, divided
2 tablespoons (30 ml) coconut oil
3 tablespoons (21 g) Sambar Podi (page 108)
1 tablespoon (5 g) ground true cinnamon
1 cup (180 g) chopped tomatoes, canned or fresh
1 can (13.5 ounces, or 378 g) unsweetened coconut milk
½ pound (227 g) spinach, stemmed and washed
Steamed basmati rice, for serving

OTHER SUGGESTED USES

Use to season Sri Lankan curries usually made with coconut milk.

Add a pinch to the filling for deviled eggs.

Add a pinch to the pan when sautéing mushrooms.

Add a pinch to tomato-based curry dishes.

1. Bring a medium pot of salted water to a boil over high heat. Add the sliced yams and cook for 5 minutes, or until half tender. Drain and cool. Combine the yams, eggplant, okra, cauliflower, and onion in a large bowl. Season with the salt, ginger, garlic, and lime juice and rub into the vegetables. Marinate the vegetables at room temperature for 30 minutes or refrigerate up to overnight before cooking.

2. Preheat the oven to 375°F (190°C, or gas mark 5).

3. Spread the shredded coconut on a baking sheet and toast until lightly browned, about 10 minutes. Cool and then combine the coconut with half the cashews in a food processor. Grind to a rough, chunky powder. Reserve the remaining cashews for garnish.

4. In a wide heavy-bottomed pot, heat the oil over medium-high heat. Cook the vegetables until crisp-tender, about 10 minutes, stirring so they cook evenly, working in two batches if necessary. Stir in the Sambar Podi and cinnamon and cook until fragrant, about 5 minutes. Stir in the tomatoes and cook a few minutes longer. Add the ground coconut-cashew powder, coconut milk, and spinach. Bring back to the boil and simmer until the sauce has thickened slightly, 3 to 4 minutes. Transfer to a serving platter and sprinkle with the reserved whole cashews. Serve over steamed basmati rice.

YIELD: 8 servings

VADOUVAN

This complex and hauntingly fragrant masala comes from Pondicherry, a former French colony on the eastern coast of India. It is based on abundant browned shallots and garlic from French cuisine combined with curry spices such as turmeric and fenugreek, and curry leaves. This home version makes a moist spice paste; other versions yield a dry spice mix in which the roasted shallots and garlic are dehydrated.

- 2 pounds (908 g) shallots, peeled and quartered
- 1 head (about 14 large cloves) garlic, peeled
- ½ cup (120 ml) vegetable oil
- ¼ cup (20 g) coriander seeds, preferably Indian
- 2 tablespoons (25 g) fenugreek seeds
- 2 tablespoons (20 g) cumin seeds
- 2 tablespoons (22 g) black mustard seeds

- 1 tablespoon (10 g) decorticated cardamom
- 1 whole nutmeg, grated (1½ teaspoons ground nutmeg)
- 3 tablespoons (30 g) ground turmeric
- 1 teaspoon freshly ground black pepper
- 1 teaspoon hot red chile flakes
- ¼ teaspoon ground cloves
- 1 tablespoon (18 g) sea salt
- 2 tablespoons (2 g) crumbled dried curry leaves

1. Preheat the oven to 200°F (95°C). Line a baking pan with parchment paper.

2. Coarsely chop the shallots and garlic using a food processor and working in batches. Pulse briefly several times until the mixture has broken down into smaller chunks. Stir once or twice and pulse again until the mixture is evenly chopped into small bits.

3. Heat the oil in a large heavy skillet, such as cast iron, then sauté the shallots and garlic, stirring often, until light golden brown, about 15 minutes.

4. Separately, heat a separate small dry skillet, then add the coriander seeds, fenugreek, cumin, mustard seeds, and cardamom and toast lightly until fragrant, shaking the pan frequently. Cool the spices to room temperature and then grind to a coarse powder in a spice grinder, blender, or mortar and pestle.

5. Combine the shallot mixture, ground spice mix, nutmeg, turmeric, black pepper, red chile flakes, cloves, and salt. Transfer to the prepared baking pan and, using fingertips, spread out thinly and evenly to a thickness of about ¼ inch (6 mm). Bake, stirring occasionally, until evenly browned, about 45 minutes, then stir and then spread out evenly again and bake for 45 minutes longer, until the mixture forms a thick paste.

6. Cool to room temperature and then add the curry leaves. Store in an airtight container in the refrigerator for up to 3 months.

YIELD: About 4 cups (900 g)

SPICEMASTER'S NOTE

Curry leaves are the small oval leaves of the tropical curry tree (*Murraya koenigii*), a member of the citrus family and native to India. The leaves, which are dark green on top and pale green underneath, run in pairs up the smaller branches of the tree. They give off their nutty fragrance with hints of anise and tangerine when bruised or rubbed. Curry leaves are essential to the vegetarian cuisines of Southern India and Sri Lanka, though they are also used in Northern India.

GRILLED VADOUVAN SALMON WITH DATE-TAMARIND CHUTNEY

Here, Franco-Indian Vadouvan, with its roasted garlic and shallot notes, seasons a side of salmon. A drizzle of syrupy sweet-tart date and tamarind chutney scented with Garam Masala accents the fish perfectly. Wild salmon is the best choice for its firm texture and distinctive flavor. If using sockeye, don't cook to more than medium-rare so it stays juicy. Frozen sockeye, partially but not fully defrosted, is a fine substitute when fresh is out of season.

½ cup (112 g) Vadouvan (page 111)
1 tablespoon (18 g) kosher salt
2 tablespoons (30 ml) vegetable oil

1 side (2 to 3 pounds, or 908 to 1.4 kg) wild salmon, preferably wild king or sockeye, trimmed and pin bones removed
Date-Tamarind Chutney

1. Preheat the oven to 400°F (200°C, or gas mark 6). Line a baking pan with parchment paper or oil the baking pan.
2. Combine the Vadouvan, salt, and oil in a bowl. Spread the mixture on the flesh side of the salmon. Place the seasoned salmon onto the prepared baking pan flesh side up and roast for about 15 minutes, or until medium-rare to medium but not fully cooked.
3. Remove the salmon from the oven. Either serve whole accompanied by the chutney or serve individual portions on top of a small pool of the chutney.

YIELD: 8 to 10 servings

DATE-TAMARIND CHUTNEY

This recipe from Mumbai is a smooth, thick, dark sweet-tart spoonable chutney made from a combination of dates and tamarind, two ingredients that have an ancient history in India. It is a standard in Indian restaurants and is served with flatbreads and legumes like lentils and chickpeas.

16 dates, pits removed, preferably large Medjools
½ pound (1 cup, or 227 g) packed dark brown sugar
1 quart (940 ml) water
1 section (2 inches, or 5 cm) fresh gingerroot, peeled, thinly sliced, and then chopped

1 cup (300 g) strained Tamarind Purée (see page 83)
1 tablespoon (7 g) Garam Masala (page 104)
1 teaspoon hot red pepper flakes
2 teaspoons (12 g) sea salt

1. Combine the dates, brown sugar, and water in a large heavy pot. Bring to a boil over high heat, and then reduce the heat to a simmer. Cook until the dates are quite soft, about 8 minutes. Add the ginger and tamarind purée and cook over low heat until thickened and dark in color, stirring often, about 15 minutes.
2. Combine the mixture in a blender until smooth or use an immersion blender.
3. Return the mixture to the pot and boil until thick enough to coat the back of a spoon (it will thicken more as it cools), about 10 minutes. Stir in the garam masala, hot red pepper flakes, and sea salt. The taste should balance sweet, salty, hot, and sour flavors.
4. Cool to room temperature in a storage container. Refrigerate up to 2 months or freeze.

YIELD: About 1 quart (900 g)

SPICED TARKA

This cooking technique and garnish from India, Pakistan, and Bangladesh, also known as *chaunk* in Hindu, uses the baghar method, often translated as "tempering," to create a hot spiced oil (see page 19 for step-by-step photos). After frying, the resulting tarka is spooned on top of bland, starchy foods such as dal (see below) and rice.

- ¼ cup (60 ml) ghee (clarified butter; vegetable oil may be substituted)
- 1 tablespoon (6 g) cumin seeds
- 2 teaspoons (7 g) black mustard seeds
- 2 teaspoons (4 g) fennel seeds
- 2 cloves garlic, minced
- 1 section (1 inch, or 2.5 cm) fresh gingerroot, peeled and grated
- 1 teaspoon asafetida

1. Heat the ghee in a small, heavy skillet. Add the dry spices—here, cumin, mustard seeds, and fennel—to the skillet. Fry briefly until they brown lightly and release their aromas.

2. Add the wet spices—garlic and ginger—to the skillet. Fry briefly until they brown lightly and release their aromas, then add the asafetida, which burns easily, and fry briefly.

YIELD: About ¼ cup (60 ml)

RED LENTIL DAL WITH SPICED TARKA

Dal, a thick purée of easily digested skinned and split legumes such as these red lentils, is a staple food eaten with rice in Southern India and Sri Lanka and with rice and roti flatbread in Northern India, Pakistan, Bangladesh, and Nepal. The Hindu word *dal* comes from the Sanskrit for "split." This simplest of poor people's vegetarian dishes is flavorful and satisfying, especially when finished with a hot spiced butter tarka. It forms an important source of vegetable protein for those eating little to no meat. Toor dal is made from yellow pigeon peas; chana dal is made from chickpeas; mung dal is made from green mung beans; and urad dal is made from black mung beans. Masoor dal, the type used here, is made from split red lentils. Split yellow peas, while not common in the India subcontinent, are prevalent in U.S. and Caribbean Indian communities, where it is simply known as "dal." Any of these legumes may be substituted for the red lentils.

- 1 pound (454 g) split red lentils
- 1 teaspoon ground turmeric
- 1 teaspoon sea salt
- 6 cups (1.4 L) water
- 1 lemon, juiced
- 1 recipe Spiced Tarka
- 1 handful cilantro, chopped for garnish

1. Combine the lentils, turmeric, salt, and water in a medium pot. Bring to a boil over high heat, then reduce the heat, partially cover, and simmer for 30 minutes, or until the lentils disintegrate into a thick, soupy purée.

2. Just before serving, add lemon juice to the dal, and then spoon on the hot Spiced Tarka and sprinkle with chopped fresh cilantro.

YIELD: 4 to 6 servings

SPICEMASTER'S NOTE

Dry spices typically used for tarka include cumin, mustard, fenugreek, black mustard, fennel, cassia, cloves, asafetida, and ajwain; fresh spices typically include onion, garlic, ginger, curry leaves, Indian bay leaves, and hot chiles.

BLENDS FROM THE MIDDLE EAST

The Middle Eastern region stretches from the Mediterranean east to Iran, north to Turkey, and south to the Persian Gulf. Early spice trade routes from China and India transversed the region to reach the Mediterranean, bringing diverse spices. Ajwain, anise, coriander, cumin, fennel, mahlab cherry, nigella, oregano, rocket, rosemary, sage, saffron, savory, sumac, and thyme are considered to be native. Coriander, cumin, mahlab cherry, nigella, sumac, and saffron are important regional seasonings. Sesame, is used in seed form or crushed into creamy tahini paste.

Other important spices originated in West or Central Asia, including asafetida, bay leaf, black mustard, dill, fenugreek, garlic, marjoram, onion, poppy, rose, and tarragon. In the Arabian Peninsula, food is seasoned with fiery blends such as Yemeni Zhoug and Hawaij, and Turkish Baharat, while Iranian Advieh relies on roses and dried limes.

Limu omani are dried, salted whole limes used frequently in Persian and Persian Gulf cooking. They can be found in Iranian and sometimes Indian grocery stores. The limes are harvested, cooked in salt water, and then oven- or sun-dried. In this state, they keep for up to two years. You can also buy limu omani in powdered form, which is easier to use in recipes. The limes come in white, dark tan, or black, with the white the most delicate form. Stronger powdered black lime is also used as an ingredient in Persian Gulf-style baharat (a spice mixture that is also called kabsa or kebsa).

IRAN

ADVIEH

Persian Advieh, cousin to Garam Masala, is a blend of five or more spices, perfumed with dried rose petals from Iran's famed Ispahan roses. Advieh for rice dishes tends to be more fragrant and is sprinkled on the rice just before serving. Advieh for *khoresht*, or meat stews, usually includes tart dried limes and generous amounts of bittersweet saffron. Advieh for pickles emphasizes spicy and tart flavors. Other common additions to advieh are star anise, angelica leaves (found in Iranian groceries), black pepper, turmeric, ginger, cloves, sesame seeds, saffron (the world's best grows in Iran, where saffron originates), and pistachios. Advieh is characterized by its sweet, delicate flavor with the haunting perfume of rose and the sharp, slightly bitter tang of dried lime.

- ¼ cup (50 g) dried culinary roses, or 2 tablespoons (16 g) culinary rose petals
- 2 tablespoons (10 g) ground cinnamon, preferably true cinnamon
- 2 tablespoons (16 g) ground nutmeg
- 2 tablespoons (12 g) ground black pepper
- 1 tablespoon (6 g) ground cardamom
- 1 tablespoon (6 g) ground cumin
- 1 tablespoon (5 g) ground limu omani

If the roses are whole, crumble them, removing and discarding everything but the petals. Combine all the ingredients. Store in an airtight container in a dark, cool place for up to 4 months.

YIELD: About ¾ cup (75 g)

WATERMELON, LABNE, AND MINT SALAD WITH LIME-ADVIEH DRESSING

The best version of this salad is made with yellow and red watermelons, here accented with tangy labne (Lebanese strained yogurt cheese) and sprightly lime-advieh dressing. The small, sweet, golden Yellow Baby melons are sometimes found at farmers' markets but are not available commercially. Most watermelons these days are bred to be seedless, which is more convenient but their texture can be mushy and their flavor dull. A firm, deeply colored melon is best here. Have a clean kitchen cloth or paper towels ready to mop up the abundant juices released when cutting the watermelon. Native to southern Africa, sweet, juicy thirst-quenching watermelons have been cultivated in Egypt since the second millennium BCE and are found throughout the Middle East, where the seeds are toasted and served as a snack with drinks.

- 1 small watermelon, preferably seedless
- ¾ cup (180 ml) extra-virgin olive oil
- 6 tablespoons (90 ml) freshly squeezed lime juice (about 3 limes)
- ½ lime, zested
- 2 tablespoons (12 g) Advieh
- ½ teaspoon sea salt

- Freshly ground black pepper
- 1 small handful spearmint leaves, shredded
- ½ small red onion, thinly sliced
- ½ pound (227 g) labne
- ½ cup (70 g) toasted pumpkin seeds (optional), for garnish

SPICEMASTER'S NOTE

Purchase food-grade or culinary roses that have not been sprayed with poisonous insecticides, or organically grown roses, or grow and dry your own.

1. Cut off the two ends of the watermelon. Pare away and discard the outer green skin of the watermelon, cutting down as far as the red flesh. Cut into two hemispheres and lay them flat side down on a work surface. Cut into slices about ½-inch (1.3 cm) thick, then cut into smaller rectangles, squares, or triangles. Pat with a paper towel to remove excess surface liquid.

2. Whisk together the olive oil, lime juice, lime zest, most of the Advieh, salt, and pepper. In a large bowl, lightly toss the watermelon pieces, spearmint, and red onion with enough of the dressing to coat generously. Arrange in a salad bowl or on individual salad plates.

3. Spoon dabs of the labne all over the top of the salad and sprinkle with the remaining Advieh and the pumpkin seeds, if using.

YIELD: 6 servings

OTHER SUGGESTED USES

Sprinkle on rice dishes after cooking.

Sprinkle on chicken and bean dishes.

Use to season meatballs and kebabs.

Use to season Persian stews called *khoresht*.

BAHARAT

Baharat simply means "spices" in Arabic and derives from the Arabic word for black pepper, which it always includes along with hot spices like paprika and chiles; sweet spices such as allspice, cloves, cassia, cinnamon, nutmeg, and cardamom; warm spices (e.g., cumin and coriander); and resinous herbs (e.g., savory and mint). Often the powdered spice blend is fried in butter, similar to the Indian tarka method of frying spices before pouring over dal. The Syrian version emphasizes allspice. Turkish Baharat includes mint, while in Tunisia, Baharat is a simple aromatic mixture of dried rosebuds, ground cinnamon, and black pepper. In the Persian Gulf region, ground limu omani (dried limes) and saffron may also be used for the spice mixture known there as Gulf baharat or kabsa.

½ cup (45 g) Pickling Spice (page 90)
¼ cup (10 g) dried savory leaf (thyme makes a good substitute)
¼ cup (6 g) dried spearmint leaves (also known as *nana* in Arabic)

3 tablespoons (24 g) black peppercorns
2 tablespoons (20 g) cumin seeds
1 cinnamon quill, preferably true cinnamon, crumbled
1 nutmeg, grated

Combine all the spices in a bowl and mix well. Grind in a spice grinder or mortar and pestle to a slightly coarse texture, working in batches if necessary. Store in a tightly sealed container away from the light for up to 6 months.

YIELD: About 2 cups (200 g)

GRILLED SIMIT KEBABS

Simit gets its name from the Arabic word *semiz,* for semolina wheat. The Greeks of Asia Minor, famed for their cuisine, brought Turkish dishes such as this back to Greece after Greek independence in 1922. One of the most important ingredients aside from the ground lamb is bulgur wheat, which binds the meat, along with ground pistachios. The kebabs are served on grilled pita bread spread with thick Greek-style yogurt and then topped with the kebabs. A side of grilled or roasted hot or sweet banana peppers and tomato halves are placed on either side with a mound of parsley, sumac, and sweet onion salad garnishing the kebabs.

FOR KEBABS
½ cup (100 g) fine bulgur
1½ cups (355 ml) water, divided
1 cup (145 g) shelled pistachios
1 bunch scallions, thinly sliced
1 small sweet onion, finely diced
6 large cloves garlic, minced
½ bunch parsley, chopped
½ bunch spearmint, chopped, or 2 tablespoons (3 g) dried spearmint

2 tablespoons (12 g) Baharat
2 tablespoons Turkish red pepper paste (30 g) or sweet paprika (12 g)
2 teaspoons Turkish Maras pepper (5 g) or hot red pepper flakes (3 g)
Sea salt and ground black pepper
2 pounds (908 g) finely ground lamb
Olive oil, for brushing

OTHER SUGGESTED USES

Use as a flavoring for lamb and beef, especially kebabs and meatballs.

Add to tomato sauce and to the filling for dolma (stuffed vegetables and stuffed grape leaves).

Use to flavor the ground lamb topping for lahmajun (Turkish flatbread "pizza").

FOR SERVING

1   small sweet onion, thinly sliced
1   large bunch Italian parsley,
     coarsely chopped
1   tablespoon (8 g) ground sumac
6   to 8 long sweet frying peppers,
     such as banana or cubanelle
6   to 8 firm but ripe tomatoes, halved
     Olive oil, for brushing
6   to 8 pita breads
2   cups (450 g) plain Greek yogurt

TO MAKE THE KEBABS:

1. Place the bulgur in a heat-safe bowl. Bring 1 cup (235 ml) of the water to a boil in a saucepan over high heat and pour over the bulgur. Leave to soften until plump, about 30 minutes, then drain.

2. Combine the pistachios and remaining ½ cup (120 ml) cold water in the bowl of a food processor and blend to a chunky paste.

3. Combine the ground pistachio paste with the scallions, onion, garlic, parsley, mint, Baharat, red pepper paste, Maras pepper, bulgur, and salt and pepper to taste. Mix well to combine evenly. Add the ground lamb and knead well until combined. Form the lamb mixture into 12 to 16 flat sausage shapes around steel sword skewers, pressing to flatten the meat and indenting the kebabs every inch (2.5 cm) or so.

4. Preheat a charcoal or gas grill until the coals are white hot and no open flames are still burning. Or preheat the broiler. Brush the kebabs with oil and grill or broil until well browned on both sides.

TO SERVE:

1. Combine the onion, parsley, and sumac in a small bowl and reserve.

2. Brush the peppers and tomatoes with oil and grill or broil. Brush the pita breads with oil and grill or toast.

3. Place the pita breads on individual serving plates. Smear with the yogurt. Top with two kebabs for each portion. Place a grilled pepper and a grilled tomato half on either side of the kebabs. Spoon the onion mixture over the kebabs and serve immediately.

YIELD: 6 to 8 servings

ZA'ATAR MIX

Za'atar is an Arabic word used to describe highly aromatic local marjoram (*Majorana syriaca*), which grows in the Eastern Mediterranean, especially Jordan, and tastes and smells like a combination of thyme (*Thymus vulgaris*), summer savory (*Satureja hortensis*), and oregano (*Origanum vulgare*). Confusingly, similarly scented herbs, including oregano, calamint (*Calamintha sylvatica*, known in Rome as *nepitella*), thyme, and savory, are also known as za'atar where they grow. By extension, za'atar is also a tangy blend of za'atar or a similar herb, tart brick-red ground sumac berries, and richly nutty toasted sesame seeds. You may substitute thyme, summer savory, oregano, calamint, or a combination of these resinous herbs for the za'atar herb.

- 1 cup (144 g) white sesame seeds
- 1 cup (50 g) dried za'atar leaves (any or all of the herbs listed above will work)
- ½ cup (48 g) ground sumac
- 2 tablespoons (36 g) sea salt

1. Heat a dry skillet over medium heat and add the sesame seeds. Toast lightly while shaking often until the seeds are golden brown and give off their nutty fragrance, about 5 minutes. Cool to room temperature.

2. Combine the toasted sesame with the remaining ingredients in a mortar and pestle and crush to a chunky, slightly oily mixture. Store at room temperature for up to 2 weeks or refrigerate for longer storage. Za'atar's flavor will begin to fade after 2 months.

YIELD: About 2½ cups (225 g)

ZA'ATAR MANOUSH

This Lebanese specialty is pita bread topped with olive oil and za'atar mix. It is usually served at breakfast often accompanied by tangy thick labne, similar to Greek yogurt. Some cooks add crushed mahlab to the dough. The stones of St. Lucy's cherries (*Prunus mahaleb*) contain small beige kernels called mahlab, which are about the size of a large peppercorn and have a distinct, bittersweet flavor reminiscent of almond extract. The soft bread rounds can be eaten either rolled up or torn into pieces and used to mop up stews or as a dipper for hummus and baba ghanoush. You may also make this bread with bread flour, though you will need to add more water.

- 1 packet (2¼ teaspoons, or 9 g) active dried yeast
- 1 tablespoon (20 g) honey
- 2 cups (470 ml) lukewarm water, divided
- 1¼ pounds (568 g) unbleached all-purpose flour, or ¾ pound (340 g) all-purpose flour and ½ pound (227 g) whole wheat flour
- 1 teaspoon sea salt
- ½ cup (120 ml) extra-virgin olive oil, divided
- ¼ cup (22 g) za'atar mix

1. In a small bowl, dissolve the yeast and honey in ¼ cup (60 ml) of the water, cover with a damp towel, and set aside in a warm place for about 20 minutes, or until the mixture is frothy.

2. Combine the flour and salt in the bowl of a mixer (or a large mixing bowl). Using the dough hook or mixing by hand, pour in the yeast mixture. Add the remaining 1¾ cups (410 ml) water as needed to form a soft dough about the consistency of pizza dough. Knead 3 tablespoons (45 ml) of the oil into the dough. Beat or knead by hand until the dough is smooth, elastic, and shiny (about 10 minutes), and then roll into a ball.

3. Rub more oil onto the inside surface of a large mixing bowl and place the dough in it. Roll around so the surface of the dough is completely coated with the oil. Cover the top of the bowl with plastic wrap or a clean, damp cloth and set aside in a warm place until the dough has doubled in volume (about 1½ hours).

4. Knock down the dough to release the gasses, then on a floured work surface roll out the dough into a long tube. Cut into 8 equal portions and form each one into a smooth ball. Flatten and stretch each ball into a round about ¼ inch (6 mm) thick. Arrange on lightly oiled baking pans, cover again, and set aside in a warm place to rise a second time until doubled in volume, about 30 minutes. Press your finger into the dough round; when the dough is ready the depression won't spring back.

5. Preheat the oven to 400°F (200°C, or gas mark 6).

6. Form indentations in each round by poking with your fingers. Brush each round liberally with more oil. Sprinkle or brush the Za'atar Mix over the top and all the way to the edge.

7. Bake the rounds until cooked through and lightly golden, about 15 minutes. Serve right away or store for later.

YIELD: 8 servings

SPICEMASTER'S NOTE

When using dried herbs, it's best to dry your own or purchase dried herbs on the branch, which are commonly exported from southern Italy and Greece. Dried herbs from a jar will likely have faded in flavor and aroma. (See page 18 for directions.)

SEVEN SPICES

Lebanese Seven Spices (also called Lebanese mixed spices) varies from family to family and from one region to another. The classic sweet-pungent blend is made of ground black and white pepper, allspice, cinnamon, cloves, nutmeg, and coriander. Another mixture known as Arabic seven spices is made from earthier spices such as cumin, paprika, and a bit of cardamom. In Syria, the mixture may include ground dried galangal, a fragrant and more pungent cousin to gingerroot used extensively in Southeast Asian cooking. Ground fenugreek, an aromatic spice common in curry mixtures, appears in some versions.

- 2 tablespoons (12 g) finely ground black pepper
- 2 tablespoons (12 g) finely ground white pepper
- 3 tablespoons (18 g) ground allspice
- 3 tablespoons (18 g) ground cinnamon, preferably true cinnamon
- 2 tablespoons (12 g) ground coriander
- 4 teaspoons (10 g) grated nutmeg
- 1 tablespoon (8 g) ground cloves

Mix all the spices and store in a tightly sealed container in a cool, dark place for up to 3 months.

YIELD: About 1 cup (50 g)

LEBANESE LAMB MEATBALLS WITH PINE NUTS AND POMEGRANATE

This tasty meatball stew, scented with Lebanese seven spice mix, consists of seasoned lamb meatballs browned and then simmered in a tangy tomato and pomegranate molasses sauce with shallots and studded with fried pine nuts. Though expensive and not easy to find, long, narrow, resinous Mediterranean pine nuts, rather than the small, pearl-shaped blander Chinese pine nuts, are authentic and delicious. The meatballs in the sauce also freeze quite well. Serve with rice pilaf, bulgur wheat, or even kasha and accompany with wilted spinach. The seltzer makes the meatballs lighter, because of the bubbles.

- 1 medium onion, grated
- 2 pounds (908 g) ground lamb
- 2 tablespoons (6 g) Seven Spices, divided
- 1 teaspoon black pepper
- 1 tablespoon (18 g) sea salt, divided
- ½ cup (120 ml) seltzer water or sparkling or plain water
- ½ cup (120 ml) olive oil, divided
- 1 pound (454 g) peeled shallots, quartered, including trimmed root end
- 2 tablespoons (15 g) all-purpose flour
- 2 cups (360 g) chopped plum tomatoes, fresh or canned
- 2 tablespoons (40 g) pomegranate molasses
- ½ cup (68 g) pine nuts

OTHER SUGGESTED USES

Use to flavor Middle Eastern meat such as kebabs, meatballs, or kibbe (bulgur wheat balls stuffed with meat).

1. Place the onion, ground lamb, 1 tablespoon (3 g) of the Seven Spices, black pepper, 1½ teaspoons (9 g) of the sea salt, and the seltzer in the bowl of a mixer. Beat to combine well (or mix by hand). Cook a small amount to check the seasonings. Using a small disher (also known as an ice-cream scoop), shape into walnut-size balls and chill until ready to cook (up to 1 day, if covered and refrigerated).

2. Heat ¼ cup (60 ml) of the olive oil in a large skillet and brown the meatballs well on all sides, working in batches. Remove the meatballs from the pan and reserve. Reserve the skillet and pour off and discard excess fat.

3. In the reserved skillet, heat 2 tablespoons (30 ml) more olive oil and then brown the shallots well. Remove from the pan and reserve.

4. Add the flour to the pan; stir to mix with the fat, and brown lightly. Add the remaining 1 tablespoon (3 g) Seven Spices and remaining 1½ teaspoons (9 g) salt, the tomatoes, and the pomegranate molasses. Bring the sauce to a boil; add the browned meatballs and shallots. Simmer together for 15 minutes, shaking the pan occasionally to keep the meatballs from sticking.

5. Meanwhile, in a small skillet, heat the remaining 2 tablespoons (30 ml) olive oil and fry the pine nuts, stirring often, until golden brown, taking care not to burn them. Stir half the pine nuts into the sauce. Serve the meatballs sprinkled with the remaining pine nuts.

YIELD: 6 to 8 servings

HAWAIJ

Hawaij is essential to the cuisine of Yemen and has spread widely into Israeli cuisine because of the large Yemenite Jewish community that emigrated there en masse in 1949 and 1950. This currylike mixture is redolent of cardamom and golden in color from turmeric. Other versions may include caraway, nutmeg, saffron, and ground dried onions. Another type, hawaij for coffee, is made from sweet aromatic spices, including aniseed, fennel seeds, ginger, and cardamom, and is used to flavor coffee as well as cakes and other desserts.

- 6 tablespoons (48 g) black peppercorns
- ½ cup (80 g) cumin seeds
- ¼ cup (20 g) coriander seeds
- 2 tablespoons (20 g) decorticated cardamom
- 2 teaspoons (3 g) whole cloves
- 6 tablespoons (60 g) ground turmeric

In a dry skillet, combine the peppercorns, cumin, coriander, cardamom, and cloves and toast over medium heat, shaking the pan often, until fragrant and lightly browned, about 3 minutes. Cool and then grind in a spice grinder or mortar and pestle. Stir in the turmeric. Transfer to a storage container and store in a cool, dry place for up to 4 months.

YIELD: About 2¼ cups (280 g)

RED LENTIL SOUP WITH YEMENITE HAWAIJ

Quick-cooking easy-to-digest split red lentils are enhanced by the warm, spicy tones of the Hawaij spice blend and an array of aromatic vegetables. This hearty lentil soup is suitable for vegans but will also be pleasing to omnivores because of its full-bodied flavor. It freezes perfectly. Like Turkish red lentil soup and Caribbean black bean soup, this soup is finished with a squeeze of citrus, here limes, which brightens the flavor.

- ½ cup (120 ml) vegetable oil
- 1 large onion, diced
- 4 carrots, diced
- 2 ribs celery, diced
- 2 leeks, diced and washed thoroughly to remove any sand
- 2 large cloves garlic, minced
- ¼ cup (31 g) Hawaij
- 2 teaspoons (12 g) sea salt
- 2 cups (360 g) chopped tomatoes, canned or fresh
- 1 pound (454 g) split red lentils
- 3½ quarts (3.3 L) vegetable stock, chicken stock, or water
- 1 bay leaf
- 3 limes, cut into quarters

1. In a large soup pot, heat the oil over medium-high heat. Add the chopped onion, carrots, celery, and leeks and sauté until the onion is lightly browned, about 8 minutes. Lower the heat to medium, add the chopped garlic, and sauté for 1 minute, or until fragrant.

2. Add the Hawaij and sauté for 2 minutes to bring out its flavor. Add the salt, tomatoes, lentils, vegetable stock, and bay leaf, and stir to combine. Increase the heat to high and bring just to a boil. Reduce the heat to low, cover, and cook at a low simmer until the lentils are tender, 35 to 40 minutes, skimming off any white foam. Taste for seasoning and serve immediately accompanied by wedges of lime to squeeze over the top.

YIELD: 8 to 10 servings

ZHOUG

This fiery green oily seasoning sauce from Yemen resembles pesto in appearance but not flavor. Yemenites believe that eating Zhoug daily keeps away illness and strengthens the heart. Some versions call for the Zhoug to be hand chopped so it is chunkier. Tomato, lemon juice, and aromatic spices such as coriander seeds, cloves, and cardamom may be added. Falafel stands throughout the Middle East, especially in Israel with its large Yemenite population, often serve Zhoug as a condiment. A little goes a long way.

½ pound (227 g) green chiles, such as jalapeño or serrano
½ bunch flat parsley, washed and dried
½ bunch cilantro, washed and dried
2 large cloves garlic, cut into smaller chunks
1 teaspoon sea salt
1 teaspoon ground cumin
1 teaspoon ground coriander
½ teaspoon ground cardamom
½ teaspoon ground black pepper
6 tablespoons (90 ml) extra-virgin olive oil, plus more to cover the top

1. Trim and seed the chiles and chop coarsely (use gloves to prevent your hands from burning when handling raw chiles). Trim away the coarse stems from the parsley and cilantro and chop the remainder, including the tender stems.

2. Combine the chiles, parsley, cilantro, garlic, salt, cumin, coriander, cardamom, and black pepper in the bowl of a food processor. Process to a rough chunky paste while pouring in the olive oil. Pack the Zhoug into a glass jar, cover the top with olive oil, and store in the refrigerator for up to 2 months.

YIELD: About 1 cup (225 g)

OTHER SUGGESTED USES

Serve with Yemenite lentil soup.

Use to season Middle Eastern–style diced tomato, cucumber, and pepper salad.

Serve with eggs instead of hot sauce.

Serve with falafel.

HUMMUS WITH WARM BUTTERY CHICKPEAS AND ZHOUG

This hummus has a satisfying nutty flavor and texture because we start with dried chickpeas. Hummus made from canned chickpeas will inevitably be mushy and on the bland side. Yes, it's more work to start with dried chickpeas, but the cost will be much less and the results much more satisfying. A small amount of baking soda neutralizes the acid in the cooking water, so the chickpeas soften as they cook. A topping of brown-butter-laden whole chickpeas adds rich texture, while the hot green zhoug provides lively herbal heat.

1½ pounds (680 g) chickpeas, soaked in cold water to cover overnight
¼ teaspoon baking soda
2 bay leaves
1 whole dried red chile (optional)
4 teaspoons (24 g) sea salt, divided
½ cup (120 ml) freshly squeezed lemon juice

4 large cloves garlic, minced
2 cups (480 g) sesame tahini
2 tablespoons (12 g) ground cumin
½ cup (112 g) unsalted butter, melted
Zhoug (page 128)
Pita bread, for serving

1. Drain and rinse the soaked chickpeas. Place in a medium pot, cover with cold water, stir in the baking soda, and bring to a boil over high heat, skimming off and discarding the large amounts of white foam that rise to the top. Add the bay leaves and whole dried red chile.

2. Cover and continue to cook the chickpeas over low heat, skimming occasionally, for about 1½ hours, or until the chickpeas are almost tender. Add 2 teaspoons (12 g) of the salt and continue to cook until the chickpeas are quite tender but not mushy. Cool and drain the chickpeas, reserving the cooking liquid. Remove and discard the bay leaves and chile pepper.

3. In the bowl of a food processor, purée two-thirds of the chickpeas along with the lemon juice and garlic. Reserve the remaining chickpeas. Add a little of the chickpea cooking liquid, only as much as necessary, to blend. Add the tahini, the remaining 2 teaspoons (12 g) salt, and the cumin and process again until the mixture is smooth, creamy, and thick enough to hold its shape.

4. To serve, mound the hummus in the center of a large, flat serving dish. Using the back of a spoon, smooth the hummus outward to create a slight hollow in the center.

5. In a medium skillet, heat the butter and cook it over medium heat until the butter browns lightly and smell nutty. Spoon the reserved whole chickpeas along with the brown butter onto the hummus. Garnish with small (very small, as it is quite hot!) dabs of Zhoug. Heat the pita bread and cut into wedges. Serve with the hummus for dipping along with more Zhoug for those who like it hot.

YIELD: 12 or more servings

NORTH AMERICAN
BLENDS

There are few common spices that are native to North America. However, the list of spice blends is much longer because immigrants from around the globe added their seasonings to the American "melting pot." Regional favorites include Chesapeake Bay Seasoning, based on the world-famous proprietary blend, Old Bay Seasoning. Hot and spicy Cajun Seasoning mix is most often used to coat and pan-sear fish. Chili Powder from the Southwest combines chiles with imported spices such as cumin, oregano, and allspice. Pastrami Seasoning came into American and Canadian culture through Romanian—Jewish immigrants. We say, "American as apple pie," so it's easy to see why a spice blend was perfected early on for this iconic dish. Similarly, the seasoning mix for pumpkin pie, a Thanksgiving favorite, soon started to be packaged by large spice companies.

APPLE PIE SPICE

This mixture of sweet spices made in many versions is used to season American apple pie. It's your choice whether to use true cinnamon from Sri Lanka, which is milder and more aromatic, or cassia cinnamon from Indonesia, which is most common in the U.S. and is hotter and more pungent.

- ½ cup (40 g) ground cinnamon
- ¼ cup (24 g) ground allspice
- 3 tablespoons (24 g) ground nutmeg
- 2 tablespoons (16 g) ground mace
- 2 teaspoons (6 g) ground cloves

Combine all the ingredients and store in a tightly sealed container in a dark, cool place for up to 4 months.

YIELD: About 1¼ cups (125 g)

SPICED APPLE TART WITH SHARP CHEDDAR PASTRY

Come fall and we start thinking apple desserts. Here the classic combination of apple and sharp Cheddar come together in a flaky tart. The Cheddar goes into the pastry and makes it easy to roll out because it is flexible. The filling is best made with tart apples that keep their shape, perhaps a combination of Fuji and Granny Smith or Honeycrisp. Apricot preserves, with its high pectin content, binds the filling and helps thicken it, adding color, body, and another layer of flavor. Sweetly aromatic Apple Pie Spice accents the pastry and filling. Serve with a dollop of crème fraîche dusted with Apple Pie Spice.

FOR PASTRY
- 10 ounces (about 2¼ cups, or 280 g) unbleached pastry flour or ½ pound (scant 2 cups, or 230 g) unbleached all-purpose flour
- ½ teaspoon fine sea salt
- 2 teaspoons (4 g) Apple Pie Spice
- 6 ounces (1½ sticks, or 168 g) unsalted butter, softened
- 6 ounces (168 g) extra-sharp Cheddar cheese, grated (about 2 cups, or 240 g, packed)
- ¼ cup (60 ml) buttermilk

FOR APPLE FILLING
- 1 cup (225 g) brown butter (see note on page 134)
- 5 pounds (2.3 kg) tart, firm apples, peeled, cored, and coarsely chopped
- 1 teaspoon fine sea salt
- 1 cup plus 2 tablespoons (225 g) sugar, divided
- 2 teaspoons (4 g) Apple Pie Spice
- ½ cup (160 g) apricot preserves
- 1 tablespoon (15 ml) vanilla extract
- ¼ cup (60 ml) dark rum
- 1 pound (454 g) tart, firm apples, peeled, cored, and thinly sliced

OTHER SUGGESTED USES

Add to apple, pear, or quince desserts, such as crisps, dumplings, tarts, and cobblers.

Add to butternut squash or pumpkin soup.

Sprinkle on acorn squash or sweet potatoe wedges before roasting.

Preheat the oven to 375°F (190°C, or gas mark 5).

TO MAKE THE PASTRY:

1. Whisk together the flour, salt, and Apple Pie Spice in a medium bowl.

2. In the bowl of a standing mixer fitted with the paddle attachment, beat the butter and cheese until well blended and creamy, 4 to 5 minutes. Add the flour mixture and buttermilk and beat just until the mixture forms a rough ball. Transfer to a plastic bag and shape into a flattened rectangle. Chill in the refrigerator for 1 hour or in the freezer for 30 minutes until firm but still malleable.

3. On a lightly floured surface, roll out the dough into a round about ¼-inch (6 mm) thick, large enough to drape over the sides of a shallow French tart pan with a removable bottom about 11 inches (28 cm) in diameter. Lay the pastry into the tart pan and press down lightly all around so the dough adheres to the pan, then trim the edges.

4. Fit a piece of heavy-duty foil onto the dough and up over the edges and fill with beans or other pie weights. Bake the crust on the bottom shelf of the oven until the dough is cooked through but not yet browned, about 30 minutes. Remove the foil and the weights, reduce the oven temperature to 325°F (170°C, or gas mark 3), and bake for 10 minutes longer, or until the dough is evenly and lightly browned. Remove from the oven and cool to room temperature on a wire rack before filling.

MEANWHILE PREPARE THE APPLE FILLING:

1. In a large heavy skillet over medium heat, heat the browned butter. Add the chopped apples and salt. Cook until the apples have started to soften, about 10 minutes, stirring often. Add 1 cup (200 g) of the sugar, the Apple Pie Spice, ½ cup (160 g) of the preserves, and the vanilla. Continue to sauté until the mixture is thick and golden, about 10 minutes, stirring often.

2. Remove the pan from the heat, add the rum, avert your head, and ignite. Place the pan back over the heat and shake it several times until the flames die out. Continue to cook the apples for 10 to 15 minutes, or until the liquid has been absorbed and the apples are tender, stirring often. Remove from the heat and cool to room temperature.

3. Raise the oven temperature to 375°F (190°C, or gas mark 5).

4. Spoon the apple filling into the prepared tart shell. Arrange the sliced apples in concentric rings on top and sprinkle with the remaining 2 tablespoons (25 g) sugar.

5. Place the tart on a baking pan to catch any drips, then bake on the bottom shelf of the oven (so the pastry cooks through) until the filling is bubbling, the pastry is golden brown, and the sliced apples have caramelized, about 50 minutes.

6. Remove the tart from the oven and allow it to cool for about 30 minutes before serving.

YIELD: One 11-inch (28 cm) tart, 12 or more servings

▶ BROWN BUTTER (BEURRE NOISETTE)

This favorite in the French kitchen is known as *beurre noisette*, or hazelnut butter, because of its toasted nut aroma. Start with 1 pound (454 g) unsalted butter. Melt the butter in a small heavy pot over medium heat. Cook until all the water cooks away, the foam on top is just beginning to color, and the milk solids on the bottom of the pan are brown and nutty-smelling. Note that when butter starts to brown, it browns quickly, so watch carefully. Remove from the heat and pour off and reserve the browned butterfat, leaving behind the small browned bits. Store refrigerated or frozen for up to 3 months.

YIELD: Makes about 1¾ cups (414 ml)

POULTRY SEASONING

This aromatic blend of resinous herbs emphasizes sage, thyme, and sweet marjoram—an often neglected herb—along with fruity black pepper and earthy white pepper plus a touch of potent, spicy-sweet cloves. Use it to season lighter meat poultry, such as chicken, capon, turkey, guinea hen, Cornish hen, and quail.

6   tablespoons (24 g) rubbed sage
¼   cup (24 g) dried thyme
¼   cup (7 g) dried marjoram
2   tablespoons (8 g) dried crumbled rosemary

2   teaspoons (4 g) ground black pepper
2   teaspoons (4 g) ground white pepper
½   teaspoon ground cloves

Combine all the ingredients, mixing well. Grind to a fine powder in a spice grinder, clean coffee mill, or blender. Transfer to a tightly sealed container and store in a dark, cool place for up to 3 months.

YIELD: About ¾ cup (56 g)

TURKEY BREAKFAST SAUSAGE PATTIES

These fresh sausages are best made from fattier dark meat ground turkey, with its full, rich flavor rather, than white meat, which tends to be dry. The sausage mix can either be hand-formed into patties or, if time allows, rolled up, frozen, and then sliced. The finer the grind, the better the sausages will hold their shape. Coarser ground meat tends to crumble when cooked.

1   medium onion, minced
2   large cloves garlic, minced
2   tablespoons (10 g) Poultry Seasoning
½   teaspoon hot red pepper flakes
2   teaspoons (12 g) fine sea salt

2   pounds (908 g) finely ground dark meat turkey
    Vegetable or olive oil, for the pan

1. Combine the onion, garlic, poultry seasoning, hot red pepper flakes, and salt in a large bowl. Add the turkey and knead to combine well. Fry up a small sample to check the seasonings. (You don't want to sample raw turkey.)
2. Shape the mixture into 8 patties by scooping first with a large spoon or a disher (also known as a an ice cream scoop) and then pressing down with your hands to form an evenly flattened disk about ½-inch (1.3 cm) thick. Firmly press an indentation into the center of the patty—this will prevent the patty from bulging when cooked. (This method also works for hamburgers.)
3. Alternatively, shape the mixture into a 2-inch (5 cm)-diameter roll. Roll it up tightly in plastic wrap, twisting the ends to enclose. Freeze until firm, then unwrap and slice into ½-inch (1.3 cm) thick rounds. Or freeze until ready to use, up to 1 month. Reserve the sliced patties covered and refrigerated until ready to cook, up to 2 days.
4. When ready to cook, heat a griddle or large skillet, preferably cast iron or nonstick, and coat lightly with oil. Add the sausage patties and brown well on both sides over moderate heat, about 3 minutes per side, until the patties are firm but still juicy. Serve immediately.

YIELD: 8 servings

OTHER SUGGESTED USES

Use to season bread stuffing for turkey.

Rub on nuts such as walnuts or pecans with a little oil and roast.

Use to season chicken or turkey burgers or sausage mix.

MONTREAL STEAK SEASONING

Montreal steak seasoning combines the British love of thick-cut beef steak with the sophisticated French flair for seasoning and perhaps a bit of Eastern European Jewish tradition with the addition of dill. Granulated garlic and onion provide the slightly gritty texture that is characteristic of this mix, but powder may be substituted. You'll find this seasoning mixture in restaurants all over the Canadian culinary capital of Montreal and anywhere that ex-pat Montrealers live.

- ¼ cup (24 g) paprika
- ¼ cup (24 g) coarsely ground black pepper (sometimes called café grind)
- ¼ cup (72 g) kosher salt
- ¼ cup (24 g) coarsely crushed coriander seeds
- ¼ cup (12 g) dried dill weed
- 2 tablespoons (20 g) granulated garlic
- 2 tablespoons (20 g) granulated onion
- 2 tablespoons (8 g) crushed hot red pepper flakes

Combine all the ingredients, mixing well. Transfer to a tightly sealed container and store in a cool, dark place for up to 3 months.

YIELD: About 1½ cups (210 g)

OTHER SUGGESTED USES

Rub on steaks, especially fatty rib steak, or skirt steak then grill.

Rub on russet potato wedges with a little oil and roast.

Brush steamed corn with butter, then sprinkle evenly with Montreal steak seasoning.

SPICED SWEET CORN PUDDING

Make this luscious corn pudding in summer when corn is at its best or use frozen corn, preferably tender white kernels. Large yellow corn will be too starchy for this dish. Substitute Chili Powder (page 142) for the Montreal Steak Seasoning if desired. Use any combination of colorful sweet and hot peppers for the batter, especially rainbow-colored farmers' market peppers in season in late summer. The sweeter and younger the corn, the more delicate and creamy the pudding.

- 3 tablespoon (42 g) unsalted butter, divided
- 1 large sweet onion (about ½ pound, or 227 g), diced
- 2 colorful sweet and hot peppers, diced
- 1 pound (454 g) shucked corn kernels and their "milk" (about 6 ears corn)
- 3 large eggs
- ½ cup (120 ml) heavy cream
- ¾ cup (180 g) Greek yogurt
- ¼ cup (56 g) unsalted butter, melted
- 4 ounces (¾ cup, or 112 g) stone-ground cornmeal
- 2 teaspoons (9 g) baking powder
- 1½ teaspoons sea salt
- 1 tablespoon (9 g) Montreal Steak Seasoning

1. Preheat the oven to 350°F (180°C, or gas mark 4). Coat a large, shallow 2-quart (2 L) baking dish with 1 tablespoon (14 g) of the butter.

2. In a medium skillet, sauté the onion and peppers in the remaining 2 tablespoons (28 g) butter until softened. Reserve.

3. Place the corn kernels in a blender or food processor. Add the eggs, cream, yogurt, and melted butter and blend. Remove the batter from blender and transfer to a large mixing bowl. In another bowl, stir together the cornmeal, baking powder, salt, and Montreal Steak Seasoning. Sprinkle into the corn mixture and stir to combine. Fold in the reserved sautéed onion and peppers.

4. Pour the batter into the prepared baking dish. Bake for 30 to 40 minutes, or until the pudding has set in the middle and started to come away from the sides of the pan. (Allow 15 to 20 minutes more baking time if using frozen corn.) Serve immediately. Store any leftovers, refrigerated, for up to 5 days. Reheat in the microwave until just steaming hot.

NOTE: If the corn is especially starchy, add 1 tablespoon (12 g) sugar and an extra ¼ cup (60 ml) cream to the batter to compensate.

YIELD: 8 to 12 servings

PASTRAMI SEASONING

Pastrami is a Romanian specialty adapted from Turkish basturma—paprika coated, spiced, pressed, and dried beef—brought to the United States by Jewish immigrants in the late nineteenth century who had picked up Turkish foodways while living throughout the Ottoman empire in places such as Salonika (Greece) and Izmir (Turkey). Dark, rich, slightly bittersweet molasses binds and thickens the mixture so that it coats the meat. Don't use blackstrap molasses, which will be overly bitter.

Rub on beef brisket or flanken (cross-cut short ribs) and leave overnight to season before hot-smoking or slow-cooking.

Rinse and pat dry a corned beef brisket. Rub generously with Pastrami Seasoning and then slow-cook in a moist environment or smoker to make your own pastrami.

2	tablespoons (16 g) black peppercorns	1	teaspoon ground cloves
2	tablespoons (20 g) white peppercorns	1	cup (320 g) molasses
		1	cup (288 g) kosher salt
¼	cup (20 g) coriander seeds	½	cup (48 g) finely chopped fresh gingerroot
¼	cup (40 g) fennel seeds	½	cup (80 g) finely minced garlic
4	teaspoons (8 g) ground allspice	½	cup (100 g) sugar

1. Combine the black peppercorns, white peppercorns, coriander seeds, and fennel seeds and grind to a slightly chunky powder in a spice grinder, mortar and pestle, or blender.

2. Combine the spices with the remaining ingredients, mixing well. Transfer to an airtight container and store, refrigerated, for up to 2 months, or freeze for up to 6 months.

YIELD: About 4 cups (1 kg)

Make grated potato and celery root latkes (fried pancakes) and top with crisp-fried shreds of pastrami.

PASTRAMI-CURED SALMON WITH HERB SALAD

Although pastrami beef is classic, rich and fatty salmon is enhanced by the same seasonings when left to cure. A variation on the Scandinavian technique of curing gravlax with salt, sugar, and dill, here the pastrami seasoning—with its salt, molasses, sugar, and spices—cures salmon, which is served in thin slices like cold-smoked salmon. It's easy to make at home, unlike cold-smoked salmon, which is quite finicky. One side of salmon will serve twelve to fifteen guests as an appetizer topped with the aromatic herb salad. It makes an impressive presentation on a buffet. Sockeye salmon, with its brilliant red color and firm flesh, contrasts beautifully with the dark cure and the bright green herb salad.

FOR CURED SALMON

1 side (2½- to 3 pounds, or 1 to 1.4 kg) wild sockeye or king salmon, with skin on

1 cup (250 g) Pastrami Seasoning

FOR HERB SALAD

½ cup (120 ml) extra-virgin olive oil

¼ cup (60 ml) fresh lemon juice

1 lemon, zested

1 large shallot, minced
Salt and pepper

1 bunch Italian parsley, leaves and small stems picked

1 small bunch basil, leaves picked; handful tarragon, leaves and small stems picked; handful spearmint, leaves and small stems picked; large handful baby arugula leaves

TO MAKE THE SALMON:

1. Remove the line of pin bones running from the head end to halfway toward the tail using needle-nose pliers (or have your fishmonger do this). Cut 3 or 4 diagonal slits through the skin. Spread the pastrami seasoning on both sides of the salmon, rubbing well so the spices penetrate.

2. Wrap in plastic wrap and place on a flat, rimmed pan, such as a jelly roll pan. Refrigerate the salmon for 3 days, turning over daily, or until the salmon is fully cured and firm to the touch. Drain off the liquid that accumulates, then pat dry.

TO MAKE THE SALAD:

1. In a small bowl, whisk together the oil, lemon juice, zest, shallot, and salt and pepper to taste; reserve. Place the prepared herb leaves in a large salad bowl.

2. Using a sharp slicing knife, thinly slice the salmon against the grain. Arrange the salmon slices in a single layer on medium or large salad plates, preferably chilled.

3. Toss the herb leaves with the dressing, using just enough to lightly coat. Arrange a small bouquet of herb salad in the center over the sliced salmon. Serve immediately. Rewrap any remaining salmon and store refrigerated for up to 1 week.

YIELD: 12 to 15 servings

BARBECUE SEASONING RUB

A rub is a mixture of finely ground spices and herbs that is vigorously rubbed into meats and poultry before slow-cooking. Rubs are most often used in barbecuing and grilling because of their ability to stick to meats during cooking. Work a generous amount of the rub into the meat up to 24 hours before cooking. Sprinkle with a second coat just before grilling or smoking.

½ cup (64 g) mild red pure chile powder, such as New Mexico, California, or ancho (not chili powder, which is premixed with cumin and oregano)
½ cup (112 g) packed dark brown sugar
¼ cup (72 g) kosher salt
¼ cup (24 g) paprika

¼ cup (24 g) smoked Spanish paprika (dulce is sweet and preferred here)
¼ cup (36 g) garlic powder
2 tablespoons (12 g) ground cumin
2 tablespoons (18 g) dry mustard powder
2 tablespoons (4 g) dried oregano
2 tablespoons (12 g) ground black pepper

Combine all the ingredients, mixing well. Transfer to a tightly sealed container and store in a cool, dark place for up to 3 months.

YIELD: About 2½ cups (400 g)

OTHER SUGGESTED USES

Rub into beef flank steak, skirt steak, or tri-tip before pan-searing or grilling.

Rub into pork ribs before slow-cooking.

Rub over chicken or turkey before roasting.

Sprinkle on buttered or olive oiled–grilled corn on the cob.

TEXAS BARBECUE BONELESS BEEF SHORT RIBS

In Texas, barbecue is all about the beef, with brisket the king of them all. These days, boneless beef short ribs, with their rich, fatty flavor, are taking over. Beef ribs are cut from various sections of the twelve ribs (plus one floating rib) that start at the chuck (shoulder) and continue to the loin. Relatively square in shape, short ribs have a full-bodied flavor and luscious melting tenderness that develops when they are rubbed with spices and slow-cooked or smoked. Although retail markets don't generally distinguish between the types, beef plate ribs from the belly (same cut as bacon) will be less expensive than fattier chuck ribs, which are known as beef chuck flap when boneless. Beef back ribs, sometimes called dinosaur ribs, will be the leanest and most expensive. Once cooked, the trimmed beef freezes well combined with the sauce.

4 pounds (1.8 kg) beef chuck flap (boneless short ribs), trimmed, or 8 pounds (3.6 kg) bone-in beef short ribs
1 cup (240 g) Barbecue Seasoning Rub
3 cups (720 g) ketchup
¾ cup (170 g) packed dark brown sugar
½ cup (120 ml) cider vinegar
¼ cup (44 g) whole-grain mustard

2 tablespoons (30 ml) Worcestershire sauce
2 tablespoons (36 g) kosher salt
½ teaspoon ground black pepper
6 large cloves garlic, minced
8 large burger buns (optional)
Thinly sliced dill pickles (optional)
Thinly sliced sharp cheddar cheese (optional)

1. One day ahead of time, rub the beef all over with barbecue seasoning. Cover and refrigerate overnight. The next day, remove from the refrigerator.

2. Combine the ketchup, brown sugar, vinegar, mustard, Worcestershire sauce, salt, pepper, and garlic in a large braiser or a slow cooker. Bring the liquid to a boil, add the beef, bring back to the boil, and then reduce the heat to very low. Slow-cook until the beef is fork-tender, about 3 hours.

3. Remove the meat from the pot and drain, reserving the sauce. Cool the beef to room temperature and then remove and discard the layer of fat from the outside. Discard the bones if using bone-in beef. Wrap and chill the beef. Separately, chill the sauce overnight in the refrigerator so the fat hardens.

4. The next day, cut the meat into small cubes. Remove and discard the hardened fat from the sauce. Bring the skimmed sauce to a boil in a wide braiser and add the beef. Heat over medium heat until the meat is thoroughly heated, about 20 minutes. Serve, spooning extra sauce over top.

5. If desired, preheat the oven to 350 degrees. Spoon the beef onto the bottoms of burger buns, top with a layer of pickle, and cover with sliced cheddar. Top with the bun lids, wrap the burgers in foil, and bake 10 minutes or until the cheese has melted. Serve immediately.

YIELD: 8 to 10 servings, about 2 pounds (908 g) cooked beef plus sauce

CHILI POWDER

Preblended chili powder was first invented to season Texas chili con carne (chile-seasoned meat). In 1890, DeWitt Clinton Pendery of Fort Worth, Texas, began supplying his blend of chiles and other spices to cafes and hotels under the name Mexican Chili Supply Company. Around the same time, William Gebhardt of New Braunfels, Texas, started making what he called Tampico Dust, which he later changed to Eagle Brand Chili Powder. The confusion over spelling is understandable. Generally when referring to the powder, the spelling is *chili*; when referring to the pepper itself, the spelling is *chile*, but other countries use a different rule and just about every variation can be found, including *chilli* (Australia).

¼ cup (40 g) cumin seeds
½ cup (48 g) ancho chile powder
½ cup (48 g) red New Mexico
   chile powder
¼ cup (8 g) Mexican oregano
   (see Spicemaster's Note, page 54)
   or Mediterranean oregano

¼ cup (28 g) onion powder
3 tablespoons (24 g) garlic powder
2 tablespoons (12 g) chipotle
   chile powder
2 teaspoons (4 g) ground allspice
1 teaspoon ground cloves

Heat a small dry skillet over medium heat and add the cumin seeds. Toast until lightly browned and fragrant but not at all dark. Cool to room temperature and then grind to a fine powder in a spice grinder, coffee mill, or blender. Combine the ground cumin with the remaining ingredients, mixing well. Transfer to a tightly sealed container and store in a dark, cool place for up to 3 months.

YIELD: About 2¼ cups (225 g)

SPICEMASTER'S NOTE

In hot weather onion powder and garlic powder tend to form hard clumps. Grind in a spice grinder to a fine powder before combining with the remaining ingredients.

COWBOY BEANS

These spicy-smoky beans are the perfect accompaniment to grilled fajita (skirt steak) or to serve on their own. Like most bean dishes, they taste even better when reheated. Serve with steamed tortillas (corn or wheat) to mop up the juices. Add the salt halfway through the cooking; if you add the salt too soon, the beans will never soften, but if you add salt after cooking, the salt won't penetrate evenly to the inside of the beans. Spoon extra beans onto tortilla chips, sprinkle with grated cheese, and toast for quick and tasty nachos.

1 pound (454 g) pinto beans
1 whole medium onion
2 whole large cloves garlic
2 teaspoons (12 g) fine sea salt
¼ pound (112 g) smoked bacon, diced
½ pound (227 g) fresh chorizo sausage, removed from casings and crumbled
1 onion, finely chopped

4 large cloves garlic, minced
6 tablespoons (36 g) Chili Powder (page 142)
1½ pounds (680 g) ripe red tomatoes, cored and diced (about 2 large)
½ small bunch cilantro, washed and chopped

1. Soak the beans in water to cover overnight with the whole onion and whole garlic cloves. Drain and rinse the beans.

2. Place the beans in a heavy pot, such as a Dutch oven. Add enough cold water to cover the beans. Bring to a boil over high heat. Reduce the heat, cover, and simmer. When the beans are half-cooked, add the salt and stir to combine well. Continue cooking until the beans are firm and almost cooked through. Fish out and discard the onion and garlic.

3. Meanwhile, in a large heavy skillet, such as cast iron, cook the bacon over low heat until most of the fat has rendered out. Add the crumbled sausage and cook until lightly browned, about 5 minutes. Add the chopped onion and minced garlic and cook until softened, about 5 minutes. Add the Chili Powder and stir to combine, then stir in the tomatoes. Bring to a boil, then reduce the heat and simmer for about 15 minutes to combine the flavors.

4. Scrape the mixture into the cooked beans and simmer together until the beans are tender and the flavors have combined, about 20 minutes, stirring often. The beans should be juicy, more like a stew than a soup. Just before serving, add the chopped cilantro and taste for salt.

YIELD: 6 to 8 servings

OTHER SUGGESTED USES

Use 1 to 2 tablespoons (6 to 12 g) Chili Powder to season 1 quart (900 g) of chili.

Add to the mix when making veggie burgers, especially those made from beans and grains.

Toss with crunchy fried chickpeas.

LOUISIANA CRAWFISH BOIL SPICES

This mixture of aromatic spices has a fiery aftertaste and is popular along the southeast coast of the United States, especially Louisiana, for boiling crawfish, shrimp, and crabs. Use the same procedure to prepare shrimp, preferably wild-caught.

½ cup (45 g) Pickling Spice (page 90)
¼ cup (72 g) fine sea salt
¼ cup (44 g) yellow mustard seeds
¼ cup (32 g) black peppercorns
¼ cup (16 g) crushed hot red pepper flakes

1 bunch chives, thinly sliced
1 piece (2 inches, or 5 cm) fresh gingerroot, peeled and finely minced
2 tablespoons (13 g) celery seed
2 tablespoons (4 g) oregano
16 bay leaves, crumbled

Combine all the spices, storing the excess in the refrigerator because of the fresh chives and ginger. Tie the spices in a muslin bag and add to the liquid for boiling seafood.

YIELD: About 3 cups (250 g)

OTHER SUGGESTED USES

Add in generous amounts to a large pot of boiling water and simmer for 30 minutes to infuse the spices. Add crawfish, shrimp, or crabs and cook.

Grind finely and use to season deviled eggs, potato salad, fish, seafood, or poultry.

LOUISIANA SPICY BOILED CRAWFISH

Crawfish are small freshwater crustaceans that look like miniature lobsters, with hundreds of species worldwide. Two important types common in Louisiana are red swamp crawfish from southern Louisiana and the white-river crawfish from northern Louisiana. Both are favorites in Creole and Cajun cooking, most often boiled in a big pot of water seasoned generously with crawfish boil spices. Serve outside on large tables covered with newspapers to crack and eat their succulent, though admittedly small, tails. Be sure to suck out the tasty juices from the head, which Cajun people know is the best part!

1   gallon (3.7 L) cold water
2   cups (240 g) Louisiana Crawfish Boil Spices (page 144), divided
4   lemons, cut in half
4   pounds (1,816 g) fresh crawfish, shrimp, or crabs, washed in cold water

1. In a large pot, combine the cold water, 1 cup (120 g) Crawfish Boil Spices, and lemons. Bring to a boil over high heat, then reduce the heat to a simmer. Cook for 30 minutes over low heat to blend the flavors.

2. Add the crawfish, stir well, and cook for 2 to 3 minutes, then turn off the heat, allowing the crawfish to poach in the hot liquid without toughening. When the crawfish are bright red and their tails are starting to curl, remove from the heat.

3. Have ready a large, clean cooler, shipping container, or other large insulated container with a lid. Place a layer of crawfish on the bottom and sprinkle generously with additional Crawfish Boil Spices. Continue layering until all the crawfish are in the container and covered with spices. Cover tightly and allow the crawfish to steam about 15 minutes or until they absorb the spice flavor.

4. Serve immediately. Provide plenty of paper towels to wipe hands.

YIELD: 8 servings

SPICEMASTER'S NOTE

Spice blends that contain paprika or ground chile powders are especially sensitive to light and will quickly fade in color if not kept in a dark place.

CAJUN SEASONING

This hot, peppery spice blend from the Cajun region of Louisiana is a favorite for making the "Cajun style" blackened fish or chicken usually prepared in a cast-iron skillet. It was originally developed as a way to flavor once abundant and inexpensive Gulf red drum fish, but now stocks of that fish are dangerously depleted, so we have substituted sustainable mahi-mahi. New Orleans chef Paul Prudhomme is often credited with bringing Cajun cuisine, especially blackened redfish, to the rest of the country and indeed the world during the 1980s.

¾ cup (72 g) sweet paprika
½ cup (144 g) kosher salt
¼ cup (24 g) ground black pepper
¼ cup (24 g) ground white pepper

¼ cup (36 g) garlic powder
¼ cup (28 g) onion powder
¼ cup (24 g) dried thyme
2 tablespoons (16 g) ground cayenne

Combine all the ingredients and store in a tightly sealed container in a dark, cool place for up to 3 months.

YIELD: About 2½ cups (250 g)

BLACKENED MAHI-MAHI

Mahi-mahi were commonly known as dolphin fish because they swim alongside boats, as do dolphins. To make the fish more acceptable to consumers, who were afraid they were eating dolphin, the fish is now known by its Hawaiian name, mahi-mahi (strong-strong), because of its great strength as a swimmer. Mahi-mahi is found mostly in Hawaii, Brazil, Costa Rica, Ecuador, Peru, the southern Atlantic, the Caribbean, and the Gulf of Mexico. Supplies are abundant because of mahi-mahi's fast growth rate. Choose smaller fish (3 to 6 pounds, or 1.3 to 2.7 kg, average) for milder flavor and finer texture; larger mahi-mahi (which may reach 70 pounds, or 31.8 kg) will be stronger in flavor with coarser texture. The creamy pink flesh is darker in larger fish and toward the tail. Its firm texture and large, moist flakes takes well to pan-searing, as in this recipe.

2 tablespoons (14 g) Cajun Seasoning
2 teaspoons kosher salt
½ teaspoons freshly ground black pepper

1 cup (235 ml) clarified butter, homemade or purchased
2 pounds (908 g) skinless mahi-mahi fillet, pin bones removed, cut into 4 to 6 serving portions
Lemon wedges

1. Combine the Cajun Seasoning and salt and pepper to taste in a small shallow casserole dish. Dip the fish fillets into the clarified butter to coat on both sides. Dip into the seasoning mixture on both sides, shaking off the excess.

2. Preheat a large cast-iron skillet until smoking hot. Add just enough clarified butter to coat the pan in a thin layer. Add the fish, starting with the outer side down, and pan-sear until well browned on both sides and the fish flakes, about 3 minutes on each side, adding more clarified butter to the pan as needed. Drain the fish and serve immediately with the lemon wedges.

YIELD: 4 to 6 servings

OTHER SUGGESTED USES

Mix with the filling for deviled eggs.

Add to tuna salad.

Sprinkle on buttered popcorn.

Add a pinch to hollandaise sauce for poached eggs.

Use to season gumbo and jambalaya.

CHESAPEAKE BAY SEASONING

This recipe, based on the world-famous Old Bay Seasoning, is a mixture of herbs and spices used to steam Chesapeake Bay's hard-shell blue crabs. The original Old Bay blend was created by Gustav Brunn, a German-Jewish spice merchant who fled the Nazis and immigrated to Baltimore in 1938, bringing with him his precious hand-cranked spice grinder and his recipes. At first he made spice blends for German-style pickles and cured meats. In 1940, Brunn came up with his own blend for seasoning crabs, which he called Old Bay Seasoning. His Baltimore Spice Company remained in the family until 1985, when it was eventually sold to McCormick & Company, the preeminent spice company in Baltimore, longtime center of America's spice trade.

SPICEMASTER'S NOTE

If you can't find ground bay leaf, you may grind your own. Crumble the bay leaves discarding any tough stems. Next, grind in a spice grinder, coffee grinder, or blender to a fine powder.

- ¼ cup (50 g) celery salt
- ¼ cup (20 g) ground bay leaves
- 2 tablespoons (18 g) dry mustard powder
- 2 tablespoons (12 g) ground ginger
- 3 tablespoons (18 g) sweet paprika
- 4 teaspoons (8 g) ground black pepper
- 1 tablespoon (6 g) ground allspice
- 2 teaspoons (4 g) ground white pepper
- 2 teaspoons (3 g) crushed hot red pepper flakes
- 2 teaspoons (6 g) ground nutmeg
- 1 teaspoon ground cloves
- 1 teaspoon ground mace
- 1 teaspoon ground cardamom

Combine all the ingredients, mixing well. Transfer to a tightly sealed container and store in a dark, cool place for up to 3 months.

YIELD: About 1½ cups (180 g)

CHESAPEAKE BAY DEVILED EGGS

When it's picnic or barbecue time, deviled eggs are an easy to make choice that everyone loves. They are inexpensive even if made using the best pastured or heritage-breed chicken eggs. Here, we season the yolks with Chesapeake Bay Seasoning. Substitute other complex, warm spice blends, such as Ras el Hanout (page 26), Chili Powder (page 142), Balti Masala (page 100), or Basic Curry Powder (page 98).

- 8 large eggs
- 1 large pinch of salt
- 1 large pinch of baking soda
- 4 tablespoons (56 g) mayonnaise, homemade or store-bought
- 1 tablespoon (7 g) Chesapeake Bay Seasoning
- 1 pinch of cayenne or other ground hot chile pepper
- 6 tablespoons finely minced chives (18 g) or scallion (36 g), divided

1. Place the eggs in a medium pot with a lid. Add cold water to cover and stir in the salt and baking soda. Cover and bring to a boil over high heat. Reduce the heat and simmer for 8 minutes or until whites are firm and yolks are mostly, but not completely set.

2. Drain the eggs and transfer to a bowl of ice water to chill. Shell the eggs, then cut them in half lengthwise. Transfer the yolks to small bowl and mash well. Mix in the mayonnaise, Chesapeake Bay Seasoning, cayenne, and 4 tablespoons of the minced chives (12 g) or scallion (24 g).

3. Spoon the yolk mixture into the whites. Sprinkle with remaining chives or scallion.

YIELD: 16 halves

OTHER SUGGESTED USES

Use to season fried fish, shellfish, chicken, and French fries.

Add to potato salad, chicken salad, or tuna salad.

Add to a Bloody Mary for a "Crabby Mary."

Add to chili or deviled eggs.

PUMPKIN PIE SPICE

This aromatic spice blend shows up in autumn in pumpkin, sweet potato, and squash pies and evokes memories of Thanksgiving. These days, it's also used to flavor pumpkin lattes, a seasonal specialty of many coffee shops. Use about 2 teaspoons (4 g) of the mix for each pie. It's your choice whether to use more delicate, floral true cinnamon or spicier, peppery cassia cinnamon, which is most common in the United States.

½ **cup (40 g) ground cinnamon**
¼ **cup (24 g) ground ginger**
2 **tablespoons (16 g) ground nutmeg**

1 **tablespoon (8 g) ground mace**
1 **tablespoon (8 g) ground cloves**
1 **teaspoon fine sea salt**

Combine all the ingredients, mixing well. Transfer to a tightly sealed container and store in a cool, dark place for up to 3 months.

YIELD: About 1 cup (100 g)

SPICED SWEET POTATO PIE

Sweet potato pie is a traditional soul food dish that originated in the cooking of American slaves, who made brilliant use of foods rejected by white owners. Here we use pumpkin pie spice to flavor the dough and the filling. Use either softer, sweeter, dark orange sweet potatoes (often known as yams) or firmer, nuttier, yellow sweet potatoes. If you have access to pure pork leaf lard, substitute it for all or part of the butter for a savory-flavored, ultra-tender crust. It's worth seeking out soft wheat pastry flour to make a tender, flaky crust.

FOR SPICED SHORTCRUST PIE DOUGH
½ **pound (2 sticks, or 227 g) unsalted butter, cut into bits and chilled**
¾ **pound (340 g) pastry flour, or a combination of ½ pound (227 g) all-purpose flour and ¼ pound (112 g) cake flour**
1 **teaspoon Pumpkin Pie Spice**
½ **teaspoon sea salt**
6 to 8 **tablespoons (90 to 120 ml) ice water**

FOR FILLING
1½ **pounds (680 g) sweet potatoes, baked until soft and then peeled**
1 **cup (225 g) packed dark brown sugar**
1 **tablespoon (6 g) Pumpkin Pie Spice**
4 **large eggs, separated**
½ **cup (112 g) sour cream**
½ **teaspoon fine sea salt**
1½ **cups (150 g) granulated sugar**

TO MAKE THE DOUGH:
1. Place the butter, flour, pumpkin pie spice, and salt in a mixing bowl. Chill in the freezer for 30 minutes. In cool weather, proceed directly to the next step.
2. Using the flat beater from an electric mixer, or by hand, cut the butter into the flour mixture until the butter pieces are the size of peas. Sprinkle the ice water over the flour mixture while tossing with your hands to distribute the water evenly.

OTHER SUGGESTED USES

Toss sweet potato slices with melted butter and pumpkin pie spice before roasting.

Sprinkle into acorn squash halves or quarters drizzled with bacon fat and then roast.

Add to pumpkin cheesecake or muffin batter.

Sprinkle on cappuccino or milk steamers.

3. Pat the mixture together until a ball is formed and the mixture holds together when a clump is pressed in your hands. If necessary, add a few more teaspoons of water, using only enough to gather in dry ingredients remaining in the bowl.

4. Using the heel of your hand, smear about one-fourth of the dough at a time across the work surface to help distribute the fat evenly in a French technique called *fraisage.* This creates long alternating strands of butter and dough that don't allow liquid to seep through. Combine the smeared dough sections into a large, flattened ball. Wrap in plastic and refrigerate for at least 1 hour to relax the gluten.

5. Roll the dough into a large circle (about 12 inches, or 30.5 cm, in diameter and ¼-inch, or 6.3 mm thick). Without pulling or stretching, pat the dough round into a 9-inch (23 cm) deep pie dish forming an attractive border and trimming off any excess dough. Chill while preparing the filling.

6. Preheat the oven to 325°F (170°C, or gas mark 3).

TO MAKE THE FILLING:

1. Cut the warm sweet potatoes into large chunks. In a large bowl, mash the sweet potatoes using a potato masher. Add the brown sugar, Pumpkin Pie Spice, egg yolks, and sour cream and mix to combine; reserve.

2. Separately, in a perfectly dry and clean mixing bowl and using a whisk or the whip attachment from a mixer, whip the egg whites (preferably at room temperature) and salt until soft and fluffy. Gradually beat in the granulated sugar and continue beating until firm and glossy. Fold into the sweet potato mixture.

3. Scrape the mixture into the prepared pie shell and bake on the bottom shelf of the oven until set in the center, about 1½ hours. Cool to room temperature, cut into serving portions, then serve with whipped cream mixed with a little sour cream for tanginess.

YIELD: One 9-inch (23 cm) pie, 8 servings

◗ RESOURCES

SUPPLIERS

Bulgarian Rose Otto
Source for dried Rosa Damascena *from Bulgaria, suitable for culinary use.* bulgarianroseotto.com/Bulgarian_dried_flowers_herbs.html

Dru Era Cinnamon
Located in Sri Lanka, this company ships true cinnamon quills and powder worldwide as well as cinnamon products such as cinnamon oil and cinnamon wood toothpicks. www.ceylon-cinnamon.com

Ethiopian Spices
Source for Ethiopian spices and spice blends such as fiery hot mitmita and mekelesha, which includes long pepper. ethiopianspices.com/html/products.asp?ItemID=1004

Fante's Kitchenware
A very knowledgeable staff at their original 9th Street Italian Market store in Philadelphia will help you find the perfect tool, jar, or pot. Look for a seemingly endless variety of kitchen tools including the oval glass spice jars seen in many of the photos in this book and a big selection of mortar and pestles. fantes.com

Indian as Apple Pie
Source for well-designed, stackable masala dabba *(container for individual spices) that makes it easy to organize your spice library.* indianasapplepie.com/products/spice-tiffin

Kalustyan's
Excellent line of spices, legumes, grains, nuts, spices, and tools—especially from the Middle East and India. kalustyans.com

Whole Spice
Freshly ground, small-batch, hand-selected, roasted, and blended spices—mostly kosher with many organic spices and herbs as well. wholespice.com

WEBSITES AND ONLINE ARTICLES

Gernot Katzer's Spice Pages
The best resource on the web for accurate information about individual spices, indexed by geography, botany, morphology, and many languages. gernot-katzers-spice-pages.com/engl/index.html

Globe & Mail
Article from the Canadian newspaper, The Globe & Mail, *about spice blends.* theglobeandmail.com/life/food-and-wine/food-trends/west-african-citrus-spice/article12814162

How to Dry Persian Limes
Make your own dried Persian limes called limu omani. ehow.com/how_5608388_dry-persian-limes.html

Making Infused Oils
This article from the University of Maine details safe and effective methods of making spice and herb-infused oils. umaine.edu/publications/4385e

New York Times
Article in the New York Times *about spices contaminated with salmonella.* nytimes.com/2013/10/31/health/12-percent-of-us-spice-imports-contaminated-fda-finds.html?_r=0

The Food Timeline
Food Timeline *with history notes, sources, and timeline for specific foods including many spices. A wonderful tool for learning.* foodtimeline.org

Veg Recipes of Indian
Extensive list of Indian spices and their names in Hindi and English. vegrecipesofindia.com/indian-spices-glossary-of-indian-spices-in-english-and-hindi/

Worldwide Metric
One of many metric converters on the internet, this one is clear and easy to use with converters for temperature, weight, length, and volume. worldwidemetric.com/measurements.html

BOOKS

Chef's Book of Formulas, Yields, and Size, by Arno Schmidt
Good resource for professional chefs and home cooks on pack sizes, counts, season, serving sizes, and even calorie counts for a large variety of ingredients. (A third edition was published in 2003, which would be more up to date.) John Wiley & Sons, New York 1996, second edition.

Cornucopia II: A Source Book of Edible Plants, by Stephen Facciola
Complete and detailed reference for every edible plant and variety. Meant for the specialist but valuable to find out just what that vegetable, herb, or fruit is along with extensive information about cultivars. Kampong Publications, Vista, CA, 1998.

Field Guide to Herbs & Spices, by Aliza Green
Compact-but-thorough guide to international herbs and spices with names in 15 to 20 languages, many unusual varieties, flavor affinities, how to purchase and store. Quirk Books, Philadelphia, 2006.

Ratio: The Simple Codes Behind the Craft of Everyday Cooking, by Michael Ruhlman
Useful for understanding the underlying proportional structure of basic recipes. Once you understand how and why recipes work, you can successfully make your own variations. Scribner, New York, 2009.

Spices and Seasonings: A Food Technology Handbook, by Donna Tainer and Anthony Grenis
Textbook covering U.S. regulations, spice processing, quality issues, spice research, and commercial production of seasoning blends. John Wiley & Sons, New York, 1993.

Spices, Salt, and Aromatics in the English Kitchen, by Elizabeth David
David presents English recipes such as spiced beef, chutneys, sauces, and fruit pickles that rely on spices and spice blends seasoned with much history, literature, and David's elegant prose. Grub Street, London, 2000.

The Book of Spices, by Alain Stella
A gorgeous coffee table book about spices from the French viewpoint with a short chapter with recipes such as *pain d'épices* and lamb tajine with prunes. Flammarion, Paris 1999.

The Cook's Guide to Spices, by Sallie Morris and Lesley Mackley
A book in the Practical Handbook series published in the U.K. Good information with a British slant about individual spices and spice blends, especially curry powders and pastes and barbecue spice mixtures. Hermes House, London 2000.

The Spice & Herb Bible: A Cook's Guide, by Ian Hemphill
The author grew up with a family in the spice business in Australia. He later opened Herbie's, a specialty spice store and online resource for top-quality spices. This man really knows his spices and herbs. Robert Rose, Toronto, 2002.

▶ ACKNOWLEDGMENTS

MY DEEPEST THANKS go to Ronit and Shuli Madrone, two Israeli-born spicemongers who carry an enormous selection of hand-selected, freshly ground, small-batch spices for their company, Whole Spice (www.wholespice.com). While working on this book, they shipped me six giant boxes of spices weighing over 100 pounds (45 kg) to do all the testing and production of the spice blends and the recipes using those blends! My list of spices started with ajwain, allspice, aniseed, annatto, and asafetida—and that's just the As.

I highly recommend their company for top-quality spices, great service, and the fact that most of their spices are also kosher. If you're ever in Napa, California, stop in to their small, well-stocked spice store at the Oxbow Market. They are especially knowledgeable and carry a large stock of hard-to-find Turkish, Middle Eastern, and North African spices such as Turkish Urfa pepper, sumac, culinary rose buds, ground Omani lime, nigella, and za'atar herb. With their generous help, I was able to make this book a reality.

I couldn't have produced this book without the assistance of friends and colleagues who helped plan, shop, prep, cook, and do the inevitable clean-up for our recipe testing and photo shoots. First, I want to thank culinary teacher Betty Kaplan who has worked with me on a half-dozen books. She worked closely with me to test all the recipes and to lead the food production for the photo shoots, even doing the shopping and prep on days that I couldn't be there. Through this and other cookbook projects, I have relied on Betty's calm and cheerful disposition, educated palate, and considered advice. The ever-energetic Linda Gellman brought her catering production experience, enthusiasm, and well-salted humor to our photos shoots. Tracy Sandberg, an artist and highly experienced caterer, brought her discerning artist's eye and meticulous technique to our last shoot, helping us to reach the highest level of photography and food quality. Young and enthusiastic foodie, Diana Zaccagnini, was generous in volunteering a day to help in the kitchen.

I've had the honor and pleasure of working with Steve Legato on just about all my cookbooks—over a dozen now. He is a consummate professional with an easy-going, warm personality who has been very appreciative of all my culinary efforts. Because of the rapport we've developed through the years, we have a fantastic working relationship with lots of collaboration and trust so that together we produce the best clear and appetizing photos while always working within a tight schedule. Here's hoping that we have the opportunity to work on many more books together!

The Giovannucci family, owners of Philadelphia's historic and beloved culinary emporium, Fante's, (www.fantes.com), provided me with a collection of glass spice jars, tools such as graters and scales, and lots of mortar and pestles—all of the quality that you only need to buy them once in your lifetime because they are so well made that they last for years and years. Everybody loves Fante's for good reason. They have everything and seem to know just about everything there is to know about kitchenware.

With this, my fifth title for Quarry Books, my thanks go to Clare Pelino, of ProLiterary Agency, for connecting me with the company in a successful, on-going relationship. Special thanks to Joy Aquilino, my editor, who has been encouraging, calming, and always there to help me make this the best possible book. Project manager Betsy Gammons always keeps me on track and full of positive energy so that together we produce a book that many will turn to again and again.

We filled the house with potent fragrances and ate a lot of aromatic, spice-laden food this past year. I felt like I was living in a spice bazaar—and I was—with all the bags and bags of spices lined up in alphabetical order on my thankfully large dining room table. Many friends, neighbors, and customers from Baba Olga's Café at Material Culture enjoyed the results of our testing. How much fun to share these dishes inspired by a world of spice blends with them and with you, the reader!

ABOUT THE AUTHOR

ALIZA GREEN is an award-winning, Philadelphia-based author, journalist, and influential chef whose books include *The Soupmaker's Kitchen*, Quarry Books, 2013, *The Butcher's Apprentice* and *Making Artisan Pasta* (Quarry Books, 2012), *The Fishmonger's Apprentice* (Quarry Books, 2010), *Starting with Ingredients: Baking* (Running Press, 2008) and *Starting with Ingredients* (Running Press, 2006), four perennially popular *Field Guides* to food (Quirk, 2004–2007), *Beans: More than 200 Delicious, Wholesome Recipes from Around the World* (Running Press, 2004) and a successful collaboration with renowned chef Georges Perrier. Green's books have garnered high praise from critics, readers, and culinary professionals alike, including a James Beard Award for *Ceviche!: Seafood, Salads, and Cocktails with a Latino Twist* (Running Press, 2001) co-authored with Chef Guillermo Pernot. Her *Making Artisan Pasta* was chosen by *Cooking Light* as one of its Top 100 Cookbooks of the Past 25 Years.

A past food columnist for the Philadelphia Inquirer, *Cooking Light Magazine*, *Prevention*, and *Clean Eating Magazine (Canada)*, Green is known for her encyclopedic knowledge of every possible ingredient, its history, culture, and use in the kitchen and bakery, for her lively story-telling garnered during a lifetime of culinary travel, and for her commitment to buying local, cooking fresh in season, and sustainably. She also leads culinary tours—her next will be to Morocco in January of 2016, where she will explore spice markets and the use of complex spice blends in the Moroccan kitchen. For more information about Aliza's books and tours, or to ask her a culinary question, visit her website at www.alizagreen.com. To send a message, click on the Ask Aliza tab.

INDEX

ALSO AVAILABLE FROM QUARRY BOOKS

MAKING ARTISAN PASTA
978-1-59253-732-7

MAKING ARTISAN CHEESECAKE
978-1-63159-054-2

LEBANESE HOME COOKING
978-1-63159-037-5